ATLANTIS IRELAND

KEYSTONE
UNIVERSITY

ATLANTIS IRELAND

ANTHONY WOODS

This book is a work of non-fiction. All punctuation and spelling is British English.

Published in 2020 by Keystone University Press.

Keystone University

www.keystone.ie

ISBN 978-1-9997288-8-5

Dedicated to those who paid the ultimate price
in the quest for wisdom

Atlantis and the ancient world as mapped by Ignacy Lelewel, 1831 - Image The Granger Collection

CONTENTS

The oak sleeps in the acorn

INTRODUCTION

The simplest things are always those the scholars see least ... the truth right under their noses - Fabre d'Olivet

The location of the legendary lost island of Atlantis is one of the greatest unsolved mysteries in human history.

Was it just an elaborate fiction given to us by the Greek philosopher Plato in 360 B.C.?

Or was there an Atlantic 'mother culture', a real place with an advanced Stone Age civilisation?

The answer is both.

The legend of Atlantis had already been passed down by word of mouth for thousands of years before Plato himself first heard it, so it's hardly surprising that some details got distorted over time. Truth became history, history became legend and legend became myth. Plato's account is exaggerated, contains historical errors and even combines two separate places into one tale. But at its heart there is a grain of truth.

When you strip back the Atlantis legend to its very core, there are three key factors:

- *The legend originated in Egypt*
- *Atlantis was a sacred island in the Atlantic Ocean*
- *The Atlantians were a 'mother culture', a Stone Age seafaring people*

Name a place on earth from Antarctica to Africa, Sweden to South America, and someone will have claimed it was Atlantis. It seems that every time someone finds so much as a brick underwater, they claim they have found the mysterious lost island. Those three vital factors - the Egyptian connection, the Atlantic location and the advanced Stone Age civilisation - are the first victims of the next fanciful claim.

Scientists roll their eyes whenever a new Atlantis theory emerges and rightly demand proof. Surely if such a megalithic mother culture existed, a civilisation which predated the Greeks and the Egyptians, then there must be some physical evidence?

For centuries, scholars have sought the missing mother culture that sowed the seeds of civilisation around the world. In recent years the evidence for this lost megalithic mother culture has become overwhelming. Stone circles have been found in virtually every country on earth. The mounds of America are the same as the mounds of Ireland. All modern languages seem to be descended from the same mother tongue. The date Plato provided for the drowning of Atlantis perfectly matches the end of the Younger Dryas Mini Ice Age period - a time of mass global extinctions and upheaval.

Academics claim Atlantis was a fable yet this doesn't stand up to scrutiny. Ancient Egyptian texts describe how their ancestors came from a sacred island in the Atlantic Ocean that was devastated in a great flood. Others claim Atlantis sank to the bottom of the ocean or it lies beneath the Azores islands. However, geologists have mapped the entire Atlantic seabed and insist this is not scientifically possible. Therefore, if the Atlantic mother culture ever did exist, there must still be evidence above ground. Something concrete, not just wild speculation.

There is a deep yearning to solve this riddle. The faded memory of Atlantis has survived more than 10,000 years because it was once a reality, a fountainhead of civilisation.

So how do we solve this riddle?

By bypassing Plato's tale altogether and going right to the source: *Ancient Egypt.*

The Egyptian civilisation predated the Greeks by thousands of years so rather than rely on Plato's useful yet unreliable tale it's much wiser to just go right to the source - Egypt.

Several ancient Egyptian texts, including *The Book of the Dead*, *The Pyramid Texts* and *The Hymn of Rameses IV* describe how their ancestors came from a sacred 'island of flame' in the Atlantic Ocean that was devastated in a great flood. Other texts refer to this ancestral territory as *Urani* - the 'sunset land' or the 'island of the setting sun'.

To this day Ireland is referred to as '*the land of the setting sun*'.

This book will provide overwhelming evidence to support the following groundbreaking claims:

- *That the Stone Age Irish were an advanced seafaring people with boats capable of international travel*
- *That Ireland is Urani - the 'sunset land' and the ancestral home of the Egyptians*
- *That the Greek legends of Atlantis and Hyperborea were both based on Ireland*
- *That the entire world, not just Ireland, has a spectacular ancient history that has been forgotten*
- *That the ancient Irish Gaelic language and ogham tree alphabet are the world's oldest*
- *That the ancient Irish Druids travelled the world sowing the seeds of civilisation*
- *That during the Dark Ages every attempt was made to remove the Druids from history for political reasons*

The author is satisfied that this book will prove beyond all reasonable doubt that the ancient Irish were a mother culture that sowed the seeds of civilisation around the world and that every country on earth, not just Ireland, has a spectacular ancient history that has been all but forgotten.

The author suggests the following three principles when reading this book:

- *Don't believe a word - do your own thinking*
- *Before you make up your mind, open it*
- *Wait for the mainstream to catch up*

The contents of this book are groundbreaking and its implications are enormous. This writing could be the ravings of a madman, the work of a genius, or anything in-between so don't believe a word you read, just do your own thinking and approach this work with an open mind. Small minds can't handle big ideas and all big ideas are viciously ridiculed and attacked. The author does not expect the ideas in this book to be accepted in his lifetime nor does he expect a rational debate on the points raised. Too many reputations are at stake and, as this work goes completely against mainstream opinion academics will snort at the very idea of *Atlantis Ireland* and label this work nonsense, gibberish, pseudoscience and so on. But a scholar has to do what a scholar has to do and nothing is more powerful than an idea whose time has come.

The current version of history is a house of cards that's about to come crashing down. The trickle of evidence for an Atlantic mother culture has become a dam that is about to burst. The author is acutely aware that when proven correct, the claims in this book will send an earthquake around the academic world and completely rewrite human history. It may take a year, a decade or even a century but this work will be proven accurate in the fullness of time. While the implications of the book are enormous, the evidence is simple and every single piece of evidence can easily be verified. References for each key piece of evidence have been included at the back of the book. Repetition is the mother of learning. Some key points are repeated throughout this book as the author weaves together many different fields of knowledge.

This is not the first time that Ireland has been cited as Atlantis. Over the centuries numerous academics have hinted at Ireland's true place in world history.

In 2004, Dr. Ulf Erlingsson, a renowned prizewinning Swedish scientist, published *Atlantis from a Geographer's Perspective* and a scientific paper which claimed that Ireland was the legendary lost island.

His claims exposed him to the scorn and ridicule of his peers who informed him that writing seriously about Atlantis was tantamount to professional suicide for an academic. Yet he went ahead anyway declaring that 'a scientist has to do what a scientist has to do.' Academics snorted at his *Atlantis Ireland* theory and experts lined up to ridicule his work. This book vindicates Erlingsson's findings and includes many additional pieces of evidence that simply weren't available when his work was published.

It's a well-known historical fact that the Egyptian civilisation predated the Greeks by thousands of years. It's also well known that Ireland's Stone Age constructions were built long before the pyramids.

A virtually unknown, yet historically proven fact is that the builders of Newgrange, one of Ireland's spectacular Stone Age temples, transported huge 5 - 10 ton boulders to the site from 30km away by boat. Part of this journey was in the open sea while the remainder was against the flow of the river. Imagine the quality of boat and level of skill required to load and unload such huge weights, let alone transport them in the open sea and against the flow of the river. The boulders are a very rare type of rock called greywacke which is only found in one place in Ireland - Clogherhead, County Louth - and could only have been transported to the site by boat in the manner outlined.

Newgrange is located at the Brú na Bóinne complex in County Meath, where around 200 unexcavated Stone Age constructions are found, including a Stone Age quay and boats. The ancient Irish clearly had spectacular boats that sailed in the open sea.

Newgrange is also perfectly aligned to the rising sun at the winter solstice, as are hundreds of Irish megaliths, which proves the early Irish had obtained a stunning knowledge of construction, astronomy, and mathematics. However, this is just the tip of the iceberg. Newgrange, Dowth and Knowth are a trinity of ancient mounds located in the Boyne Valley. At the winter solstice the sun projects its golden rays into Newgrange at dawn and into Dowth at sunset. Not only are Ireland's majestic mounds aligned to the movements of the sun, they are also aligned to each other. Knowth is one of Ireland's best-kept secrets. It's the largest mound on the Emerald Isle and is aligned to the spring and autumn equinoxes. Sundials, early calendars, and megalithic art depicting the path of the moon across the night sky are found carved into Knowth's huge kerbstones. Hundreds of similar alignments are found all across the Emerald Isle. To the ignorant, these are meaningless coincidences, to the wise they are stunning proof of an advanced Stone Age civilisation.

We know for sure that the Stone Age Irish were master astronomers. We know for sure they had boats in the open sea. It's not much of a stretch to imagine they explored the wider world using the stars for direction.

With wild forests, wild animals and wild people to contend with, travelling over land was a very dangerous business and up until very recently in human history sailing was by far the safest and most practical form of transport. The sea was not the obstacle it appears to modern man, it was the primary means of travel and idea transfer for thousands of years. The sea once dominated human life and boats were the aeroplanes of the time

Stone Age man was also a lot more mobile than he has been given credit for. Recent scientific breakthroughs prove that man sailed to Australia on rafts 65,000 years ago shattering the previous illusion that Australia was only first inhabited a few centuries ago.

The stereotypical Irish combination of red hair, blue eyes and milky-white skin is the rarest genetic combination on earth. Less than 0.1% of the global population possess this genetic combination. Around the entire world we find legends of a mysterious red-haired, blue-eyed race who brought with them the gifts of civilisation while red-haired mummies have been found all over the world, including in New Zealand, China, Peru, Alaska and Egypt. Thousands of fair and red-haired mummies have been found across Egypt. The Egyptian Pharaoh Ramesses II had red hair, as did at least six other pharaohs. The legendary Cleopatra is also said to have had red hair.

Our ancestors were also a lot more intelligent than they have been given credit for. Take for example the precession of the equinox, the observable phenomenon of the rotation of the heavens, also known as the Great Year cycle which spans a period of 25,920 years. Knowledge of this cycle was known to the ancient Egyptians, Greeks and Hindus. Knowledge like that could not possibly be developed over a few centuries or even a few millennia - knowledge like that takes *tens of thousands of years* to develop. Man is much older than we realise.

Examine ancient history with an open mind and the trail leads back to Ireland. The mounds of America are the same as the mounds of Ireland. Druid stone circles are found in virtually every country on earth proving that the entire world, not just Ireland, has a spectacular forgotten ancient history. The mysterious megalithic builders have left their mark all over the globe and their constructions have unmistakable similarity. The most spectacular Stone Age constructions on earth are found in Ireland.

Archeology is like a silent movie however, only language can provide the soundtrack. Study the ancient languages of the world including Hebrew, Arabic, Chaldean and Sanskrit and you will be stunned by the similarities with old Irish Gaelic. Several scholars over the centuries have claimed that Irish Gaelic is the world's oldest language and that ogham, the tree alphabet of the Druids, was the world's first alphabet.

In Joseph Gwilt's timeless masterpiece *The Encyclopaedia of Architecture*, he informs us that standing stones predated all other forms of architecture, that the Druids were the world's first race of civilised people, and that at one time the language and alphabet of the entire ancient world from Ireland to India was the same - that of the Irish Druids.

By all scales of development what man has achieved in the last few thousand years is truly staggering. For over three million years early man has fumbled around with stone tools yet, in the space of just a few thousand years humans are flying to the moon and sending probes deep into space. What was the spark that triggered this rapid advancement?

A *mother culture* - the first humans to climb out of the slime of ignorance and develop a civilisation that was ahead of its time. These same people travelled the world sowing the seeds of civilisation, not to build an empire but to push the human race forward. This book will prove to the impartial observer that Ireland was the base of this Atlantic mother culture and the fountainhead of civilisation. You will also learn how parts of Ireland have been flooded by tsunamis several times in the past and how a giant tsunami drowned Atlantis Ireland.

Greek history contains a detailed record of how Pythagoras, who predated Plato by almost a century, was taught by an Irish Druid called Abaris, who could speak fluent Greek as if he had spoken it all his life. The ancient Irish annals confirm that an Irish Druid called Abhras visited Greece, amongst other places, on his travels. The Greeks described how Abaris was from the mystical island of Hyperborea, which just like Atlantis, was another name for Ireland.

Hercules and Perseus, two of the most important characters in Greek mythology, were both said to have visited Hyperborea, which was described as being a fertile island to the north of Gaul (France) with a circular temple (Newgrange) and priests with harps. According to the Greeks, Hyperborea was governed by the Boreades. In Irish, *boreadach* means noble chieftain. Clearly, Ireland is the Greek Hyperborea.

The later Greeks, such as Aristotle, called Ireland '*Ierne*', which means *sacred island.*

Aristotle spoke of a *sacred island* in the Atlantic called Ierne.

Plato spoke of a *sacred island* in the Atlantic called Atlantis.

Diodorus spoke of a *sacred island* in the Atlantic called Hyperborea.

All were descriptions of Ireland clouded by mythology, superstition and a primitive knowledge of geography. Several Latin writings refer to Ireland as '*Insula Sacra*' which also means *the sacred island* while over time Hyperborea became Hybernia or Hibernia, the Roman name for Ireland.

That the Romans undertook a campaign of vicious persecution and destruction against the Druids is a well-known historical fact. Arles in the south of France contained an ancient Druid college that was founded around 2,000 BC. This Druid college was completely destroyed by a Christian mob in 270 AD.

In 389 AD another large Druid college in Bibrate, France was also destroyed by a Christian mob. This college had an astonishing 40,000 students and offered courses in philosophy, literature, grammar, law, medicine, astronomy, architecture and religion.

The opinion of Aristotle that philosophy came to the Greeks from the Gauls (Druids) is very striking.

While Britain and France were strongholds, Ireland was the source of Druidism, a philosophy that predated Rome, Greece and Egypt by millennia. Every attempt was made to delete the Druids from history, in particular by the Romans as they furiously destroyed the libraries, schools and temples of the ancient world, including the Great Library of Alexandria in Egypt, acts which plunged the world into the Dark Ages. During this time, Ireland's reputation was dragged through the mud by *two bloodthirsty empires* hellbent on global domination.

One of the greatest secrets of human history is that all the world's religions and civilisations have their roots in one mother soil - Irish Druidism - a master philosophy that predated and influenced all the others.

As hard as it may be for those ignorant of Irish history to accept, the Irish were an old civilisation when the Greeks were still young. For example, the Irish Tailtean games predated the Greek Olympics by over 1,000 years, while the Irish Brehon laws are the oldest laws on Earth.

The Egyptians were old when the Greeks were young, but the Irish Druids were older still.

There can be no doubt that Ireland's history was written by her enemies. For the best part of 1,000 years, Ireland's culture has been desecrated, her books burned, and her ancient language driven to the point of extinction. Her reputation has been dragged through the mud while some of the most deplorable acts of brutality and genocide ever committed on earth were committed on the Emerald Isle by the very people who wrote Ireland's history. It's time to set the record straight.

If this book is right then the world's academics are wrong and hell hath no fury like an academic scorned. The high priests of academia will line up to ridicule this work and label it quackery, pseudoscience and gibberish. This book is not written for their approval - it's written for the freethinkers of today, the scholars of tomorrow and generations not yet born.

Sixteen years ago, a brave Swedish scientist claimed that Ireland was Atlantis. Hopefully, we don't have to wait this long for the mainstream to catch up, but if we do, so be it. The Irish have waited over a thousand years to clear their name. Another decade won't make any difference.

No other place on earth has the ancient history, mythology or culture of Ireland. The Stone Age Irish had boats capable of carrying 10-ton boulders, a truly astonishing feat of engineering.

It's ignorant to think the wandering Irish didn't use these boats to explore the wider world.

A ship is safe in the harbour but that's not what a ship is for

Newgrange, Brú na Bóinne, Ireland - Front Elevation

Newgrange, Brú na Bóinne, Ireland - Side Elevation

Dronehenge, Brú na Bóinne, Ireland - Image Anthony Murphy

Artist's impression of Dronehenge, Brú na Bóinne, Ireland

New discoveries at Newgrange - National Monuments Service Ireland

Knowth, Brú na Bóinne, Ireland - Image Anthony Murphy

Irish Stone Age boat reconstructed using only traditional methods and tools - Image Boyne Currach Heritage

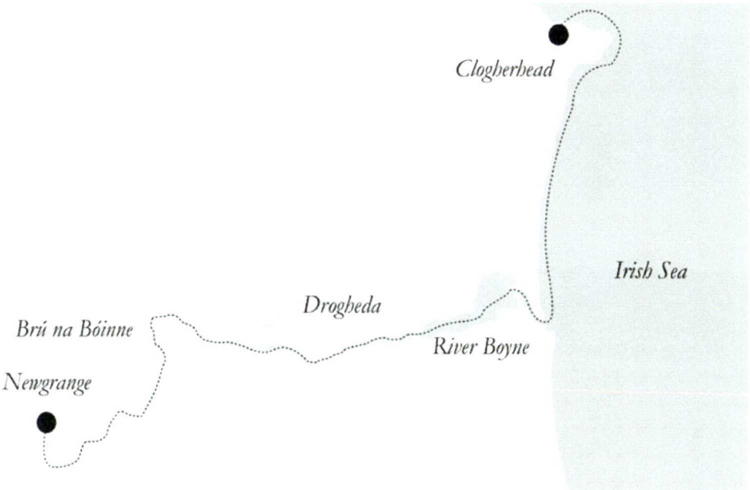

30km boat journey from Clogherhead to Newgrange with 5 - 10 ton boulders.

EGYPT

Reserve your right to think, for even to think wrongly is better than not to think at all - Hypatia

Egyptian texts describe how their ancestors came from a sacred 'island of flame' in the Atlantic that was devastated in a great flood. These texts, including *The Egyptian Book of the Dead, The Pyramid Texts* and *The Hymn of Rameses IV*, also tell of ten kings who ruled during the reign of the gods. In the Pyramid Texts we find this interesting reference :

Those who come with their bodies full of magic, from the Island of Flame

One of these was Thoth, the founder of the Egyptian civilisation, who was born in a distant island in the west, a country which was across a body of water. This 'island of flame' or 'mound of fire' was described as being the 'first land' and site of the sacred 'primeval mound'. Stone age Ireland is synonyms with sacred fires, mounds and sun worship. Other texts refer to this ancestral territory as the 'sunset land' or the 'island of the setting sun'. To this day Ireland is referred to as 'the island of the setting sun'. Another name for this land in Egyptian texts was Urani, which is etymologically very close to *Éireann*, Ireland's ancient name.

According to Egyptian texts, this island in the Atlantic was overwhelmed by water and 10 kings, including Thoth, travelled east to safety by boat. These records tell how the founders of Egypt arrived from an island in the Atlantic around 12,000 years ago.

Pharaoh King Menes is widely accepted as being the founder of the First Dynasty. Towards the end of his life Menes sailed seeking the sunset land, the ancestral home of the Egyptians. When archaeologists opened his Egyptian tomb, it was found to be empty, his body was elsewhere. A hieroglyphic text found by Sir Flinders Petrie in 1901 in his empty tomb says:

'King Menes, the Ruler of Mizraim [Egypt] made the complete course to the end of the Sunset Land. Sailing in ships, he completed the inspection of the Western Land. He built there a holding in Urani Land. At the Lake of the Peak, fate pierced him by a Hornet (Bee Sting) . . . This drilled tablet set up of hanging wood is dedicated to his memory.'

Here we have proof that the ancestral home of the Egyptians, known as Atlantis in mystical circles, was above water and visited by a pharaoh who died and was buried there. The final resting place of Pharaoh Menes was discovered in Knockmany, County Tyrone, Ireland by explorer Laurence Waddell who wrote about his discovery in in several books including *The Makers of Civilization* and *Egyptian Civilization* which contain original photographs of stone carvings from the site. He also described how linear writing on a boulder stone at the site was almost identical with that found in the pharaoh's empty Egyptian tomb.

It seems that Egyptian Pharaoh Menes is buried in Ireland although the site has never been excavated to confirm this find. Nor, indeed, has Scotia's grave in County Kerry, which is widely accepted as being the resting place of an Egyptian pharaoh's daughter who arrived in Ireland around 1700 B.C. In fact, very few of Ireland's ancient sites have been excavated. It must be the most unexcavated place on earth. However, some startling evidence has been found at the handful of sites that have actually been excavated. The 3,800-year-old remains of youth wearing Egyptian faience beads was found at the Hill of Tara, the ancient seat of Ireland's High Kings. Stone tools dating back 200,000 - 400,000 years have been found in three separate sites across Ireland while the 2,300 year-old skull of a Barbary ape, a small monkey native to North Africa was found at Navan Fort in County Armagh.

Hidden deep in the Egyptian desert we find the most unexpected thing - a stone circle. The Nabta Playa complex is considered the origin of Egyptian astronomy and the *birthplace* of Egyptian civilisation itself. The remarkable Nabta Playa complex is a timeless memorial of a long-forgotten people that *predated* the spectacular Egyptian civilisation that followed. The entire area contains stone circles, mounds and burial chambers, as well as megalithic and carved standing stones. So far, around 30 of these structures have been uncovered at the site.

Nabta Playa is located in one of the most extreme climates on earth and is isolated in every direction by baking desert. Around 11,600 years ago the African Humid Period brought water into the region. Nabta Playa once had regular rainfall, seasonal lakes and a landscape suitable for early agriculture.

This site provides evidence of a society *not previously recorded* in ancient Egypt - a forgotten people. These overlooked megalithic structures remain the most valuable remnants of a lost Egyptian culture. The burial mounds, astronomy and agricultural knowledge found at Nebta Playa prove that it was here the seeds of Egyptian civilisation were first sown by a forgotten people.

In the earliest Egyptian writings we find several references to mounds including:

The gods...who live in Horus's mounds, who live in Seth's mounds

A mound to the sky will be pounded for him

That far palace of the lords of kas in which the Sun dawns from the Horus Mounds and the Seth Mounds

There can be no doubt that the mound was a sacred structure to the earliest Egyptians just as it was all around the world. In the Egyptian pyramid texts the 'Benben' was said to have been a mound that arose when the earth was first created on the 'island of flame'. As the Egyptian civilisation developed the construction of mounds evolved into the building of pyramids.

The earliest settlements at Nabta Playa had domesticated cattle. Among the earliest Egyptians, cattle were central to their belief system and regarded as earthly representatives of the gods. The sun was sometimes referred to as the *Bull of Heaven* and his divine mother (the universe) was called the *Cow of Heaven.* The ancient Irish also honoured cattle and described the Milky Way as the *Way of the White Cow.* The roots of the spectacular Egyptian civilisation are found in the sacred soil of Ireland - the Egyptian land of the setting sun.

As a side note, ancient Egyptian texts describe a second sphinx that is buried beneath the sands of Giza and how both sphinxes are connected by a walkway of initiation that leads underneath the Great Pyramid. The entrance to this walkway is found between the paws of the Sphinx and is sealed by a concrete slab. This second Spinx is buried 70 feet below ground level underneath the recently built helipad. Also, one of the most precious historical jewels on earth - the lost labyrinth of Egypt - is thought to lie just 100km away in Hawara. This labyrinth is believed to surpass even the majesty of the great pyramids and is thought to hold many priceless lost historical records. Neither site has ever been acknomledged yet rumours of them persist. In 2008 a team of scientists led by Louis de Cordier claimed to have discovered the labyrinth using ground penetrating radar. The author leaves these clues as a treasure map for the inquisitive mind.

There are many genetic links between ancient Ireland and Egypt. The stereotypical Irish genetics of red hair, blue eyes and milky-white skin is the rarest genetic combination on Earth. Less than 0.1 % of the global human population possess this mix of recessive traits. For the record, when red hair is described throughout this book it is a reference to the range of colours between fair - strawberry blond - fiery red - auburn - reddish brown.

Ireland has the highest concentration of red-haired genetics in the world. Throughout history, pockets of redheads have been found scattered across the globe in the unlikeliest of places. These are the descendants of the ancient Irish and include the Hebrews, Phoenicians, Berbers and Indo-European Aryans while red-haired mummies have been found all over the world, including in New Zealand, China, Peru and Alaska.

One of the most famous Egyptian mummies in the world is housed in the British museum in London. This mummy, which dates to around 3400 BC, has earned the nickname 'Ginger' because of his red hair. Ginger is not an isolated case - thousands of fair and red-haired mummies have been found across Egypt.

The Egyptian Pharaoh Ramesses II had red hair, as did at least six other pharaohs. Despite claims to the contrary, it has been conclusively proven that Ramesses' hair was naturally red. The legendary Cleopatra is also depicted as having red hair.

In the *Egyptian Book of the Dead* we find this interesting reference to a mummified god with red hair:

Chebt the mummified form of the god, the greatly beloved, with red hair

Over time the early bringers of civilisation became known as gods, a pattern common all around the world. Because they were more advanced they appeared god-like with their technology, language and dress. Hunter gatherers were astonished by people who could domesticate cattle, grow crops and communicate using language. The chariot was a particularly awe-inspiring object to early man and in numerous traditions, gods are depicted as riding in chariots.

Further genetic evidence backs up the Ireland/Egypt connection. In genetics, a haplogroup is a group from the human family tree that traces back to one individual ancestor. The highest concentration of Pharaoh Tutankhamun's Haplogroup R-M269 found anywhere on earth is found in Ireland and 70% of Irish men carry this haplogroup while less than 1% of modern Egyptians do. R-M269 is found all along the Atlantic coast of western Europe. Tutankhamun genetics are *Atlantic European.*

The Egyptians were unquestionably the most advanced civilisation of their time and the majesty of the pyramids is a timeless testament to their achievements. This book merely points out that civilisation did not start nor end with the Egyptians. With red-haired pharaohs, stone circles and sun worship it's obvious there is a big connection between the ancient civilisations of Egypt and Ireland.

While the Egyptians were old the Irish Druids were older still and Egyptian texts confirm the roots of their civilisation are found in the sacred island of Urani, the land of the setting sun - Ireland.

The Sun, gives all things life and fertility. It is the true god of the earth
- Napoleon Bonaparte

Nabta Playa Stone Circle, Egypt - Image Aswan Nubia Museum

Wassu Stone Circles, Gambia, Africa

The highest concentration of Tutankhamen's 'Atlantic European' DNA Haplogroup RM-269 is found in Ireland

GREECE

It is better to change an opinion than to persist in a wrong one - Socrates

The ancient Greek writers make frequent mention of a nation of people called the Hyperboreans who lived on a sacred island in the Atlantic. Hyperborea was described as being a fertile island to the north of Gaul (France) with a temperate climate, very fertile soil, a circular temple (Newgrange) and priests with harps.

According to the Greeks, the Island of Hyperborea was governed by the Boreades. *Boreadach* is an old Irish word which means noble chieftain or wise leader. Clearly, Ireland is the Greek Hyperborea.

Greek history contains a detailed record of how Pythagoras learned from a mysterious traveller called Abaris the Hyperborean. Ancient Irish records confirm that an Irish Druid called Abhras visited Greece, amongst other places, on his travels. The Greeks described Abaris as a legendary sage, healer and prophet who could speak fluent Greek as if he had spoken it all his life. Abaris came from the sacred island of Hyperborea, which, just like Atlantis, was another name for Ireland. Pythagoras, one of the smartest men that ever lived learned from an Irish Druid. Here we have proof of an incredibly high state of learning in the land of Abaris - Ireland.

Atlas, the first king of Atlantis lived among the Hyperboreans while in the earliest Greek writings the sacred Garden of Hesperides, also known as the Garden of Atlas, was located in Hyperborea, the sunset land in the west. In later writings the Garden of Atlas was located in North Africa.

Hercules and Perseus, two of the most important characters in Greek mythology, were both said to have visited Hyperborea and Hercules had a son with a Hyperborean woman. The Greek goddess Leto, the mother of the Apollo was also a Hyperborean.

Swans feature in several Greek myths about Hyperborea. The Greeks describe how the Hyperboreans celebrated their god in a festival of music, song and dance whose hymns were joined by the sweet song of the circling swans. These beautiful birds also play an integral part in Irish mythology and feature heavily in the most important legends and poetry. The Irish who have left the island, and their descendants, are known poetically as the wild geese. A wild goose is a swan.

To this day a flock of swans live at the Newgrange mound, one of Ireland's most sacred sites. In one Greek legend, the Hyperborean people are transformed into swans after bathing in certain waters, similar to one of the most famous of all Irish legends - *The Children of Lir*.

Just like in Ireland, mound-building was a key part of early Greek culture. There are numerous mounds, locally called tumuli, found all over Greece. It was common to raise a mound for a significant person upon their death. Several Greek poems describe how a huge mound or tumulus was raised over the bones of the Greek hero Achilles. Incidentally, Achilles was depicted as having golden or red hair.

Wolves are heavily associated with both Hyperborea and Apollo's mother, the goddess Leto. Greek legends describe how the pregnant goddess Leto came from Hyperborea to the island of Delos accompanied by a pack of wolves, where she gave birth to the Greek sun god Apollo. This interesting quote is found in Greek writings:

Wolves are not easily delivered of their young, only after 12 days and 12 nights, for the people of Delos maintain that this was the length of time that it took Leto to travel from the Hyperborea to Delos.

The early Irish domesticated native wolves and large hounds which over time became the famous Irish Wolfhound, while 12 days would seem a reasonable timeframe to sail from Ireland to Greece.

After Leto gave birth to Apollo in Delos, the Hyperboreans sent pilgrims - five men and several maiden-priestesses. However, after several of the maidens were either raped or killed the Hyperboreans ended the pilgrimage and instead delivered their annual 'first fruits of the harvest' offerings, which were wrapped in wheat, indirectly through neighbouring tribes. These gifts came from the western ocean - the Atlantic.

The oracle of Delphi - the most sacred site in ancient Greece - was founded by three prophets from the sacred island of Hyperborea who took up residence there. The Greeks called these prophets Pagasis, Agyeus and Olen which is a corruption of the three ranks of Irish Druid - *Bag-ois*, *Agh-is* and *Ollam.*

Several stories describe the Hyperboreans as the pilgrim-founders of other important Greek shrines. In Ireland, a Druid was considered a wise man or woman, a philosopher, law giver, scientist and astronomer.

In the earliest Greek mythology, the Garden of the Hesperides containing the sacred tree of golden apples was located in Hyperborea while in later writings it was located in North Africa. There are numerous legends of sacred trees and golden apples in the ancient Irish annals including 'the golden apples of Lough Erne', 'the golden apples in the land of promise' and 'the golden apples of the fairies'. Even the golden apples of the Hesperides themselves are mentioned in an Irish legend involving Lugh, (pronounced Lu) - a key figure in Irish mythology. In wider Celtic mythology, portrayals of Lugh usually show him holding three apples representing immortality, prosperity and power. Lugh is considered a solar deity and was a member of the *Tuatha Dé Danann,* a highly advanced people in Irish mythology who were known as 'the shining ones' or 'the tribe of the gods'. The DéDannans were similar to the Greek Olympians and were considered a mortal yet divine race. In one legend thc DéDananns are said to have arrived in Ireland in *ships from the sky*, in another they arrived in clouds without ships. Greek philosopher Pythagoras met the wandering DéDananns while they were on their travels.

The Druid Abhras was also a member of the *Tuatha Dé Danann.* In *The Round Towers of Ireland* by Henry O'Brien, we find this reference to the wandering DéDananns, and specifically to Abhras the Druid, visiting Teneas, a long-lost ancient Greek city that was only discovered by archaeologists in 2018:

The purport of the Tuath-de-danaans journey was in quest of knowledge,

And to seek a proper place where they should improve in Druidism.

These holy men soon sailed to Greece …

Morfios and Earus-Ard, **Abhras**, *and Lemas, well-skilled in magic,*

Were the names of our Druids;

they lived in the reign of Garman the Happy.

Morfios was made Fele of Falias, Earus the poet in Gone dwelt,

Samias dwelt at Mhurias, but **Abhras**, *the Tele-fionn, at Teneas.*

The Hyperboreans also appear in the myths of the founding of the Olympic Games. It was said that when Hercules (Herakles) established the festival in honour of Zeus, he made a pilgrimage to Hyperborea to obtain sacred wild olives for the shrine. The Irish Tailtean games predated the Greek Olympics by over 1,000 years and there are ancient Irish records of Greek merchants attending this festival and selling merchandise. When the Olympics were first founded, they used the same by-laws that the Irish games had been using for centuries.

Let us examine and translate some excerpts taken from writings of Greek historian Diodorus in his *Library of History (Book II Chapter 47)* where he described the sacred island of Hyperborea and its people.

There is an island in the ocean over against Gaul (France) … where the Hyperboreans inhabit;

There is an island in the Atlantic Ocean near France … where the Hyperboreans live

The soil here is very rich, and very fruitful; and the climate temperate, insomuch as there are two crops in the year.

This island has a temperate climate, very fertile soil and can produce two crops per year

They say that Leto was born here, and therefore, that they worship Apollo above all other gods;

Leto, the mother of Apollo (Greek Sun God) was born here and they worship the sun above all other gods

Apollo's priests, who has there a stately grove and renowned temple, of a round form, beautified with many rich gifts.

The Druids have a beautiful woodland and a circular temple made beautiful with gifts

There is a city consecrated to this god, whose citizens are most of them harpers, who, playing on the harp…

There is a city dedicated to the sun whose residents are mostly harpers who while playing the harp…

Chant sacred hymns to Apollo in the temple, setting forth his glorious acts.

In the temple hymns are chanted to honour the sun and his glorious acts (daily defeat of the darkness, annual death and resurrection)

The Hyperboreans use their own natural language

They have their own ancient language (old Irish Gaelic)

Of long and ancient time have had a special kindness for the Grecians, and more especially for the Athenians and them of Delos.

They have a special ancient bond with the Greeks, particularly with inhabitants of Athens and Delos

Some of the Grecians passed over to the Hyperboreans, and left behind them divers presents, inscribed with Greek characters;

Some Greeks visited Hyperborea and left behind gifts inscribed with Greek writing

And that Abaris formerly travelled thence into Greece, and renewed the ancient league of friendship with the Delians.

Abaris the Druid visited Greece and renewed the ancient bonds with Delos

Apollo once in 19 years comes into the island; in which space of time the stars perform their courses and return to the same point

The sun god visits the island every 19 years when the stars have completed the 19-year cycle of the moon

And return to the same point; and therefore the Greeks call the revolution of nineteen years the Great Year.

This 19-year cycle is called the metonic cycle - the Great Year of the moon

At this time of his appearance (they say) that he plays upon the harps, and sings and dances all the night from the vernal equinox

They say when the sun god visits the island, he plays the harp, sings and dances every night from spring

To the rising of the Pleiades, solacing himself with the praises of his own successful adventures.

To the appearance on the horizon of the Pleiades - a cluster of seven stars said to be the daughters of Atlas

The sovereignty of this city, and the care of the temple (they say) belongs to the Boreades

The Boreades are the people responsible for the leadership of this city and the care of the temple

Hyperborea was governed by the Boreades. *Boreadach* is an Irish word which means 'noble chieftain' or 'wise leader'. It can also mean 'judge'. In more recent times magistrates in Ireland were often called *Boreadhas.* Ireland is clearly the Greek Island of Hyperborea.

Diodorus described the *sacred island* of Hyperborea.

Plato described the *sacred island* of Atlantis.

Aristotle described the *sacred island* of Ierne.

All were descriptions of Ireland clouded by mythology, superstition and a primitive knowledge of geography.

The opinion of Aristotle that philosophy came to the Greeks from the Gauls (Druids) is most striking.

While France and Britain were Druid strongholds, Ireland was the source of Druidism, a philosophy that predated Egypt, Greece and Rome by millennia. Every attempt was made to delete the Druids from history, in particular by the Romans as they furiously destroyed the libraries, schools and temples of the ancient world, including the Great Library of Alexandria. These crimes set humanity back thousands of years.

This destruction of light and learning plunged the world into a dark age that was designed to forever hide a great secret that was never again supposed to see the light of day, a secret so powerful it could topple the Roman Empire and rewrite human history:

All the world's religions have their roots in Irish Druidism - a master philosophy which predated and influenced all the others.

The Druids travelled great distances from the Emerald Isle and had schools all over the ancient world. Arles in the south of France contained an ancient seat of learning founded by the Druids around 2,000 BC. This Druid college was completely destroyed by a Christian mob in 270 AD.

In 389 AD another large Druid college in Bibrate, France was also destroyed by a Christian mob. This college had an astonishing 40,000 students and offered courses in philosophy, literature, grammar, law, medicine, astronomy, architecture and religion. The value of the knowledge lost by such atrocities is truly priceless.

The Druids and Pythagoreans both taught the *immortality of the soul* - that there was a divine immortal part of man - the soul - trapped in an animal body - the beast - and it was man's task to overcome the temptations of the lower self to develop wisdom, also known as gnosis or enlightenment. The Christian Gnostics (who predated the Vatican by centuries) also taught a similar philosophy as did several other 'pagan' cultures across the ancient world. In eastern teachings this process was described as raising the kundalini or 'taming the serpent within'. The soul was described as the higher self, the higher mind or the wisdom within while the lower self or lower mind was known as the animal within. The ancients taught that true virtue and wisdom came from conquering the lower animal mind. The word 'soul' is derived from the Irish world *solas* which means light, as is the world *sol* which means sun. To the ancients the soul was *the sun within*, a pure spark of the divine fire.

The Hyperboreans were renowned harpers and the priests of Hyperborea played harps - the national instrument and official symbol of Ireland. The Greek god Apollo, who lived among the Hyperboreans, gave Orpheus a magical harp or lyre. In Irish, *orpheam* is the ancient name for a harp. Orpheus was a Greek hero who was said to have been the author of sacred writings. He described the sun as the 'eye of heaven'. He was also a renowned musician, poet and prophet best known for his ability to entrance all things including wild beasts with his music.

The Greeks described an ancient order of priests called Orpheans who *travelled a greater part of the world* to instruct in divine matters. The Orpheans were *Druids.*

The Greek Pherenicus describes the Hyperboreans *as being of the ancient blood of the Titans* and described how they had two distinct Atlantic colonies - *one in Europe to the north (Ireland), the other opposite at the extreme part of Africa (Mauritania).* The early Greeks had a primitive knowledge of geography compared to today and these two related Atlantic locations - Ireland and Mauritania - were combined many times in Greek records.

The Greek word Atlantis literally means 'the island of Atlas'. Atlas was the Greek Titan who bore the heavens on his shoulders and was a very important character in Greek mythology who personified the quality of endurance. The expression *carrying the weight of the world on your shoulders* comes from the legend of Atlas, while in modern day psychology an Atlas personality is found in someone who was forced to take on excessive responsibilities during childhood. According to the Greeks, Atlas was the first king of *two separate places* - the island of Atlantis and Mauritania, Africa. The Atlas Mountains in North Africa and the Atlantic Ocean are both named after Atlas.

According to early Greek mythology *Atlas lived on the sacred island of Hyperborea* which was also the location of the Garden of Hesperides, a mystical garden that contained a sacred tree bearing golden apples. This apple tree was given by the earth goddess Gaia to the Queen of the Olympians on her marriage to Zeus - the king of the Greek gods. The Garden of the Hesperides was also known as the *Garden of Atlas* or the *orchard in the west.* In Greek mythology, both gods and mortals coveted the golden apples because they promised immortality. Anyone who ate them would never again experience hunger, thirst, suffering or illness.

The sacred tree with its golden apples was tended by the beautiful golden-haired daughters of Atlas who were called the *Atlantides.* They were also called 'the goddesses of the evening', 'the Hesperides' or 'the nymphs of the west'. In one legend we are told how Hercules as part of his 12 labours reached Atlas who was among the Hyperboreans and asked him to fetch the golden apples before tricking him and leaving with the prize. In another legend the golden apples were associated with a Greek heroine called *Atalanta.*

The sacred apple tree and its forbidden fruit was guarded by a large serpent dragon called Ladon. Interestingly the *Garden of Atlas* had forbidden fruit, females and a serpent just like the *Garden of Eden.*

Atlas had many children, mostly daughters, which were collectively referred to as the *Atlantides.* Zeus, king of the Greek gods and Maia - a daughter of Atlas - had a child, the Greek messenger god, Hermes.

Hermes is an extremely important character in Greek mythology and references to Hermes are found in the very earliest Greek writings. As a descendent of Atlas, Hermes was described as an *Atlantiades* and is heavily connected with stone cairns (piles of rocks) and also the mystical *Emerald Tablets of Atlantis.* Hermes also visited Hyperborea and was the equivalent of the Egyptian god Thoth - the founder of the Egyptian civilisation who left his ancestral home in the sunset land, an island in the Atlantic, which was destroyed by a great flood.

Atlas was the first king of *two separate places* - the Island of Atlantis and Mauritania, Africa.

Today Mauritania is mostly desert but only a few thousand years ago it was a rich fertile land with an abundance of crops, gold and ivory. Located in Mauritania near the Atlas Mountains is the Richat Structure, a huge naturally-occurring circular structure that at one time was surrounded by lakes, fertile lands and was connected by river to the Atlantic Ocean. At one time this huge structure, which is also known as the Eye of the Sahara, had three concentric rings of land and water and is what remains today of the lost city of Atlantis.

The Eye of the Sahara in Mauritania Africa is what remains of the Lost City of Atlantis (not the island)

This structure was known to the Greeks as the ancient city of Cerne, and was an early Irish settlement in Mauritania, Africa. Cerne is derived from the Irish word *cairn*, which means stacked or piled rocks. Cairns have been used from the most ancient of times as forts, landmarks and sacred sites.

Interestingly, in Greek history the name Cerne actually referred to *two separate places:* an African city near the Atlas Mountains and an island in the Atlantic Ocean that was 12 days' sail from the Straits of Gibraltar.

Similarly, Plato's Atlantis was a combination of the same *two separate places:* the island of Atlantis (Ireland) and the City of Atlantis (city of Cerne/the Eye of the Sahara, Mauritania).

In Greek mythology Atlas was the first king of *two separate places:* the island of Atlantis and the kingdom of Mauritania, Africa.

The Greek Diodorus, in his *Library of History (Book III, Chapter 54)*, describes how the Atlantians were a civilised people who had a settlement called Cerne near the Atlas Mountains and that it was here that the warlike Amazons, a ferocious army of female warriors from Libya, slaughtered the Atlantians before attacking Greece and waging war in the region. Greek history is very consistent in supporting the account of Diodorus, but not that of Plato, that it was actually the Amazons who attacked Greece and waged war in the region, not the Atlantians.

Myrina first attacked the Atlantians in the city of Cerne - Diodorus

Beyond the Pillars of Heracles there is an Island (Atlantis) - Plato

Beyond the Pillars of Heracles Are Two Islands ... Albion (Britain) and Ierne (Ireland) - Aristotle

In Greek mythology, Helios carries the sun across the sky every day in a sun-chariot. One day his son Phaethon takes control of the sun-chariot and its four powerful horses. Almost immediately though, there are problems as Phaethon cannot control the horses, and the chariot veers upwards and downwards violently. When the sun chariot travels too high, the earth starts to freeze, but when it plunges downwards, the planet starts to burn. To restore order Phaethon is struck down and cast from heaven by Zeus, sending his flaming body plummeting into a *Hyperborean* river.

Most epic mythology like this is written in the stars - it's an attempt to explain celestial events by story. The tale of Phaethon seems like an attempt to explain extreme climate events, while a comet striking earth would appear to early man as a god being cast out of heaven. As an interesting side note, Phaethon was also the name given to a missing fifth planet that is claimed to have once existed between the orbits of Mars and Jupiter. According to this theory, the planet exploded after a huge catastrophe and the asteroid belt is all that remains of it today. This planet was also called Lucifer or Maldek in some old writings that claim it thronged with life and its explosion is said to have showered the earth with a swarm of comets. The theory of a missing fifth planet has been around for centuries and many great astronomers supported it while many others didn't. The main objection to the theory is the total combined mass of the asteroid belt is too small to make a planet however, this is a poor explanation - just as a detonated bomb leaves very little residue, if a planet did explode you wouldn't expect much to remain apart from a few asteroids. If a planet did indeed explode it would appear to early man as a god being cast out of heaven or a fallen angel. There is currently no definitive proof that the asteroid belt was once a planet and most scientists claim it's merely the remains from the formation of the solar system. Time will tell whether the asteroid belt was once a planet - either way, it's a very interesting theory that would make a great movie.

Hyperborea is heavily connected with the legend of Phaethon. Plato's famous legend of Atlantis started with the tale of Phaethon, both of which were first heard from the ancient Egyptians as follows:

There have been, and will be again, many destructions of mankind arising out of many causes; the greatest have been brought about by the agencies of fire and water, and other lesser ones by innumerable other causes.

There is a story that even you (the Greeks) have preserved, that once upon a time, Phaethon, the son of Helios, having yoked the steeds in his father's chariot, because he was not able to drive them in the path of his father, burnt up all that was upon the earth, and was himself destroyed by a thunderbolt.

Now, this has the form of a myth, but really signifies a declination of the bodies moving in the heavens around the earth, and a great conflagration of things upon the earth, which recurs after long intervals.

Plato was one of the greatest minds of all time and, like many other great philosophers, he often *concealed hidden meanings* in his writings. It is interesting that he started his tale of Atlantis with a story directly related to Hyperborea, Phaethon and a great catastrophe on earth. Perhaps this was a clue.

The most telling characteristic of Plato's Atlantis is that it was an island located in the Atlantic Ocean. Ireland is an island in the

Atlantic with an ancient people, language and culture. There are an estimated 100,000 Stone Age constructions remaining in Ireland including the most spectacular megaliths on earth, just as you would expect if they really were an advanced early civilisation. Similar constructions (mounds, cairns, stone circles, dolmens, passage tombs, and so on) are found all over the planet, proving that the entire world, not just Ireland, has a stunning and forgotten ancient history.

Some claim that Atlantis lies at the bottom of the ocean or beneath the Azores. However, science has eliminated these suggestions as a possibility. Geologists who have mapped the entire Atlantic seabed are adamant that a large sunken island in the Atlantic is not scientifically possible.

Plato famously said that Atlantis was *swallowed by the sea in one unfortunate day and night.* A tsunami is a much more practical explanation for the drowning of Atlantis and an island in the Atlantic that does exist is a much more viable explanation than an island that doesn't.

During Plato's time the Greeks had absolutely no idea where Ireland/Atlantis/Hyperborea was, and Ireland didn't appear on any of their maps for quite some time afterwards. We are dealing with a period in history when the world's first maps were only just being developed. Errors about the location of a mystical island far away in the Atlantic that drowned almost 10,000 years beforehand are to be expected.

There are many descriptions of Plato's Atlantis that perfectly fit Ireland, while there are also many that don't. It's clear that Plato's legend is useful but unreliable, that it combined two separate related places, a lot of exaggeration and several historical errors. Yet at its heart is a grain of truth.

Plato's Atlantis was an island in the Atlantic with a fertile, circular plain which was surrounded by mountains that descended towards the sea. Ireland is the only island on earth with these features. There are also many details in Plato's description that fit like a glove - the steep cliffs on one coast, the gentler slopes on the other coast and a fertile central plain that has a view to the sea while being encircled by mountains.

Plato never described Atlantis as a continent, only an island. The continent aspect of the legend is a recent addition. Similarly, the Egyptians described the sacred *island* of their ancestors in the Atlantic, not a continent.

Plato's Atlantis, just like Hyperborea, had a temperate climate capable of producing two crops per year. Ireland has one of the most temperate climates on earth and to this day is capable of producing two crops a year: winter and spring barley. Meanwhile, Ireland's Ceide fields are the world's oldest agricultural fields.

Plato's Atlantis had many hot and cold springs. Ireland has 27 warm springs and thousands of cold ones, known locally as holy wells.

Plato's tale also described the spectacular city of Atlantis, a huge circular city with an abundance of elephants, gold and ivory. This is a reference to the ancient city of Cerne, an early Irish settlement in Mauritania, Africa.

The site of the city of Cerne is Plato's lost city of Atlantis. It is also known as the Eye of the Sahara or the Richat Structure.

In Greek history the name Cerne referred to *two separate places:* an African city in Mauritania near the Atlas Mountains and an island in the Atlantic Ocean that was 12 days' sail from the Strait of Gibraltar.

Similarly, the Hyperboreans had a settlement in Mauritania and a sacred Atlantic island that was 12 days' sail from Greece. Again, we note *12 days' sail* and *two separate places* combined into one legend.

Plato's Atlantis was a combination of the same *two separate places*: the island of Atlantis (Ireland) and the city of Atlantis (city of Cerne/the Eye of the Sahara, Mauritania).

In Greek mythology Atlas was the first king of *two separate places*: the island of Atlantis and the kingdom of Mauritania, Africa.

Plato's tale described how Atlantis was 'swallowed by the sea' - this was a reference to a giant tsunami. Ireland has been impacted by several tsunamis over the millennia including a large one around 6,000 years ago however the giant tsunami that completely drowned the island was caused by a comet impact in the Atlantic ocean near the Puerto Rico trench - a truly cataclysmic event that triggered huge global upheaval.

Plato's tale also described the sinking of the island of Atlantis. As the sea level has risen around 120m since the end of the last Ice Age, a large part of what was once Ireland is now underwater and there is a sunken landmass and forest off the east coast of Ireland that is thought to be at least 6,000 years old, if not much older.

The Storegga Slides mega-tsunami and the sinking of Doggerland were probably also merged into the legend of Atlantis by early man, events which happened in the same region of Europe several thousand years later. The Storegga Slides were a serious of enormous underwater landslides in the Norwegian Sea around 8,200 years ago which resulted in a mega-tsunami that affected Ireland, Britain and Northern Europe. This tsunami and associated subsidence would have decimated the local Stone Age populations and deposited huge quantities of debris into the Irish sea making it impassable, just like Plato's Atlantis.

At the time of the Storegga Slides, Ireland was the only large island off the coast of Europe and Africa. Britain was not an island at this time - it was attached to mainland Europe by a large landbridge known as Doggerland which linked Britain, Denmark and the Netherlands. A thriving Stone Age culture once lived in this rich hunting and fishing region. Many artefacts have been found in Doggerland including a carved spearhead made from an antler which is almost 14,000 years old. Ancient tree stumps, flint tools and the fossilised remains of a mammoth all help form a picture of how Doggerland's landscape once looked. It was very low-lying and was permanently submerged by rising sea levels after the Ice Age ended. There is no doubt it would have been heavily impacted by a mega-tsunami triggered by the Storegga Slides. That was probably the last time it was above water.

Although this is not the same event that drowned Atlantis Ireland, it's easy to see how they got combined in the tale - both were devastating tsunamis affecting the same region in the very distant past. The Storegga Slides tsunami occurred 8,200 years ago, while the tsunami that drowned Atlantis Ireland occurred around 11,600 years ago. Ireland was also impacted by another large tsunami around 6,000 years ago. Several Irish place names record these events, including *Díseart Tola* in County Clare which means *desert of the flood.*

Some speculate that Doggerland and Britain, not Ireland, was Atlantis however, this is not the case for several reasons. Firstly, neither are in the Atlantic Ocean, secondly, Britain was not an island when Atlantis was drowned around 11,600 years ago and thirdly, it was the Irish that bought civilisation to Britain from the west. Britain's west coast has a much higher concentration of Stone Age megaliths than its east coast as clear evidence for this claim. Study a map of European megaliths and its obvious the builders came from the west by sea, from Atlantis Ireland where the most impressive Stone Age constructions on earth are found.

Plato described how the kings of Atlantis ruled their own island and many surrounding lands. According to an old Irish text called the *Lebor Gabála Érenn*, Úgaine Mór, the 66th High King of Ireland, also ruled the entire island of Britain in or around 300 BC. Perhaps the true history of the Irish partly explains the fury with which Britain attacked her people, burned her ancient books, and drove her ancient language to the point of extinction.

Ireland has a very temperate climate due to the Atlantic Gulf Stream. This warm ocean current did not stop during the Great Ice Age or the Younger Dryas (mini Ice Age) period. Ireland has been habitable for hundreds of thousands of years, not just the last

10,000, an outdated view of stale historians who still think Ireland was entirely frozen over during the Ice Age - a view that has been discredited by modern science.

Plato provided the measurements of 3000 x 2000 stadia for Atlantis in the following paragraph:

The whole country was described as being very lofty and precipitous on the side of the sea, but the country immediately about and surrounding the city was a level plain, itself surrounded by mountains which descended toward the sea;

It was smooth and even, and of an oblong shape, extending in one direction three thousand stadia, but across the centre inland it was two thousand stadia

A stadia is 166m and is equal to 200 megalithic yards - a megalithic yard is 0.829m. From its furthest points, which is how land was measured up until very recently in history, Ireland measures 2,932 x 2,038 stadia.

When we multiply the *length x width* of both, the total area is virtually identical:

Atlantis - 3000 x 2,000 = 6,000,000

Ireland - 2,932 x 2,038 = 5,975,416

Using these figures, Ireland is within 1% of Plato's measurements and is the only large island on earth that's even close.

Plato also described how the circular temple of Atlantis was half a stadia wide.

Half a stadia is 83m. The circular Newgrange temple is 85m wide - an almost perfect match.

The observant reader will recall that in Greek records, the Hyperboreans also had a circular temple. This is yet another reference to Newgrange. The legends of Atlantis and Hyperborea are both based on Ireland. Let us now examine and translate some more of the words Plato used to describe Atlantis.

Beyond the Pillars of Heracles there lay an island

There is an island in the Atlantic Ocean beyond the straights of Gibraltar

3000 stadia long and 2000 stadia wide

The island of Ireland measures 2932 x 2038 stadia at its furthest points - within 1% of Plato's measurement

The kings of the islands of Atlantis once had an extent larger than Libya and Asia put together

The scale or reach of the kings of Atlantis was global - bigger than all of Africa and Asia combined

And was the way to other islands and from those islands you might pass through the whole of the opposite continent

Ireland was a stepping-stone to sail to Iceland, Greenland and on to the opposite continent - America

A circular Temple to Poseidon with a strange barbaric appearance and measuring a half stadia wide (83m)

Newgrange in Ireland's Boyne Valley measures 85m in diameter, an almost perfect match

Located 50 Stadia from the Sea

Newgrange is 50 stadia (8.3km) from the sea. A Stone Age quay and boats have been found near Newgrange.

9000 years before the time of Solon

Around 11,600 years ago - the end of the Younger Dryas/mini Ice Age period

In a great disaster

A great disaster struck. Disaster is a Greek word which means 'evil star' - such as a comet striking the earth & the resulting tsunami

In a single day and night ...the island of Atlantis was swallowed by the sea

The island of Ireland was suddenly engulfed by a huge tsunami

In the centre of the island was a plain surrounded by mountains which is said to have been the fairest of all plains and very fertile

In the centre of Ireland is a great plain that is surrounded by mountains. It's probably the most fertile plain on earth.

Though fair the sight of Erin's plains, hardly will they seem so after you have seen the great plain... a wonder of a land, the land of which i speak
- Tochmarc Etaine

Greek mythology describes a race of giants who lived in Hyperborea. To this day Ireland is known as the *Land of Giants* and in Irish mythology we find many references to the Fomorians - a race of seafaring giants with strong links to Africa where they were known as the Formiae, a giant people who formed settlements in Libya. In Irish legends the Fomorians inhabited Ireland before the great flood and were said to have been as old as the hills. In some accounts they were described as being sea pirates who were troublesome to the whole world. Another Irish legend describes how after a huge battle involving the Fomorians, the sea rose and drowned most of the participants, just like Plato's legend of Atlantis, but a handful survived on higher ground while 30 also escaped to Britain, Greece and the 'Northern islands' of the world. According to Irish records, the descendants of the survivors who went to Greece were called *Fir Bolg* (the Bag Men) as they were enslaved by the Greeks and made to carry bags of construction materials. After 230 years of slavery they left Greece (around the time the Israelites are said to have left Egypt) and sailed in a great fleet to Iberia (Spain) and then on to Ireland.

According to Plato the Atlantians attacked Greece however this view is not supported by any other Greek text. The Greek Diodorus, in his *Library of History*, describes how the Atlantians were a civilised people who had a settlement called Cerne near the Atlas Mountains and that it was here that the warlike Amazons, a ferocious army of female warriors from Libya, slaughtered the Atlantians before attacking Greece and waging war in the region.

Myrina first attacked the Atlantians in the city of Cerne, and when she took the city she killed all the adult males, enslaved the women and children, and razed the city - Diodorus

Greek history is very consistent in supporting the account of Diodorus, but not that of Plato, that it was actually the Amazons, not the Atlantians, who attacked Greece and waged war in the region. It seems likely that the version of the tale Plato himself first heard had confused the Amazons of Libya with the nearby Atlantian settlement in Mauritania.

Most people when they think of Atlantis, they think of a sunken island far beneath the sea, yet science has ruled this out as a possibility. There is also the strong possibility that the sunken island myth was intentionally created by the early Irish simply to protect the island by stopping people looking for it. At the time, the world was an extremely bloodthirsty place and disinformation was a great tactic to avoid invasion. If you thought someone was likely to break into your home, would you tell them where you lived?

Interestingly, the ancient Irish annals do contain a detailed record of an *attempted invasion of Ireland by the Greeks and Romans* who were defeated at the Battle of Ventry in County Kerry. This attempted invasion does not appear in any Greek or Roman texts, only the ancient Irish records. Perhaps it's here, on Ireland's wild Atlantic shoreline, that Rome's famous missing Ninth Legion met their demise.

For a man to conquer himself is the first and noblest of all victories

- Plato

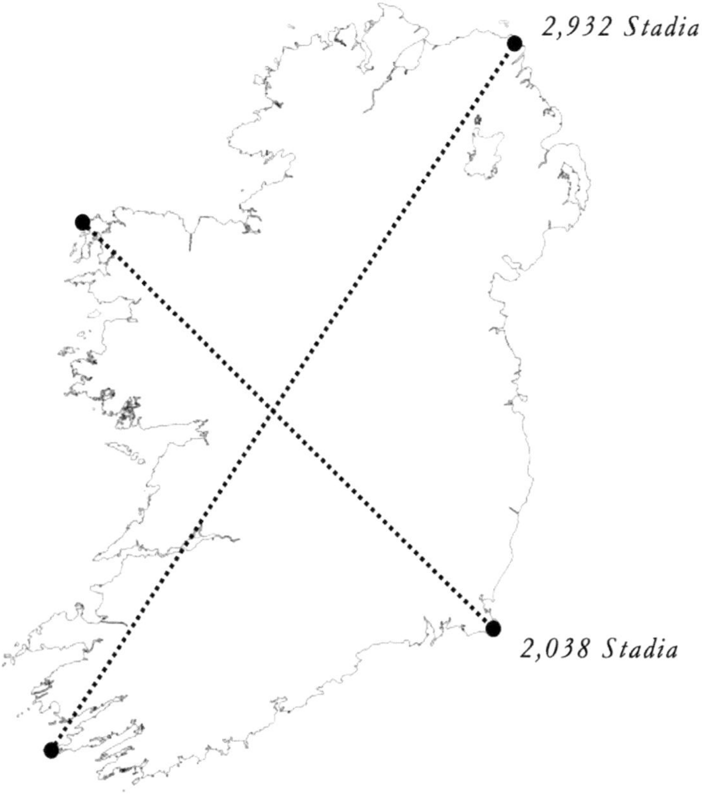

Plato's Atlantis was 3,000 x 2000 stadia.
Ireland is 2,932 x 2,038 - within 1% of Plato's measurements

The 40km-wide Eye of the Sahara in Mauritania, Africa - Image George Steinmetz

Artist's impression of Plato's City of Atlantis

AFRICA

Education is the most powerful weapon which you can use to change the world
- Nelson Mandela

Plato's legend of Atlantis described a fabulous circular city with concentric circles of land and water. If the city Plato described was ever in Ireland *Brú na Bóinne* is the most likely location. It contains a Stone Age quay, hundreds of unexcavated circular structures and the spectacular Newgrange temple. There are also dozens of alternative possible locations around Ireland and there is also the possibility that a Stone Age city once existed in what now lies beneath the waves along Ireland's coastline. Just off the Dublin coast in the Irish sea near Bray, a 6,000-year-old underwater forest is visible leaving no doubt of a submerged landscape on Ireland's east coast. This submerged land contained hills, marshlands and river valleys and is an unexplored region in which any evidence of early human activity is still likely to be preserved.

There are also several old Irish legends from the west coast that describe how a great part of Ireland was swallowed by the sea and how the sunken part often rises to be seen on the horizon. One such legend involves the island of *Hy-Brasil*, a mystical island said to be located off the west coast of Ireland in the Atlantic. Another legend describes a place called *Tir-Hudi* which contained a spectacular ancient city which once possessed all the riches of the world. Clearly both echo Plato's legend of Atlantis.

However, the city Plato described had an abundance of elephants, ivory and massive quantities of gold. There is only one place on earth that matches that description - Africa - and just like the Greek legend of Hyperborea, Plato's legend of Atlantis combined the same two separate places and a lot of exaggeration into one spectacular tale. In order to prove the *Atlantis Ireland* theory, it certainly would be a lot easier for the author to simply ignore the Eye of the Sahara and Africa entirely, however the truth is the truth, no matter how inconvenient.

Plato described a large circular city with concentric circles of land and water with an abundance of elephants, gold and ivory. This is actually a reference to an ancient Irish settlement in Mauritania called Cerne, sometimes spelt Kerne in Greek writings. The name Cerne is derived from the Irish word *cairn* which means 'pile of rocks'. The city of Cerne was located at the base of Mount Atlas in Mauritania, Africa in a structure called the Richat Structure or the Eye of the Sahara.

Just like Plato's description of the city of Atlantis this huge structure consists of three concentric circles and has a disused spring in the centre island. It is also an incredible 40km wide. The structure is hidden on three sides by the spectacular Atlas Mountains and is near a huge flat plain with hundreds of thousands of acres that was once abundant with life. Today it is a barren desert.

In Greek history the name Cerne actually referred to *two separate places,* an African city near the Atlas Mountains and an island in the Atlantic Ocean that was 12 days' sail from the Strait of Gibraltar.

Early Greek accounts of Hyperborea placed it in the sunset island in the Atlantic while later legends combined the same *two separate places* - Ireland and Mauritania.

Similarly, Plato's Atlantis was a combination of the same *two separate places*: the island of Atlantis (Ireland) and the city of Atlantis (city of Cerne/the Eye of the Sahara, Mauritania).

The Greek Diodorus, in his *Library of History*, describes how the Atlantians were a civilised people who had a settlement called Cerne near the Atlas Mountains and that it was here that the war-like Amazons, a ferocious army of female warriors from Libya, slaughtered the Atlantians before attacking Greece and waging war in the region. Diodorus also tells us that a city inhabited by the Amazons in the large nearby lake (Tritonis) disappeared during an earthquake. The following are some excerpts from his writings:

Now the Atlantians, dwelling as they do in the regions on the edge of the ocean and inhabiting a fertile territory, are reputed far to excel their neighbours in reverence towards the gods and the humanity they showed in their dealings with strangers, and the gods, they say, were born among them.

Atlas received as his part the regions on the coast of the ocean, and he not only gave the name of Atlantians to his peoples but likewise called the greatest mountain in the land Atlas. They also say that he perfected the science of astrology and was the first to publish to mankind the doctrine of the sphere.

Near the salt is a mountain called Atlas, very taper and round; so lofty, moreover, that the top (it is said) cannot be seen, the clouds never quitting it either summer or winter. The natives call this mountain 'the Pillar of Heaven'; and they themselves take their name from it, being called Atlantes. They are reported not to eat any living thing, and never to have any dreams.

The Amazons were afflicted by an urge to attack the greater part of the inhabited world.

The Amazons embarked upon great ventures, a longing having come over them to invade many part of the inhabited world.

The first people against whom they advanced, according to the tale, was the Atlantians, the most civilised men among the inhabitants of those regions, who dwelt in a prosperous country and possessed great cities.

Now the queen of the Amazons, Myrina, collected, it is said, an army of thirty thousand foot-soldiers and three thousand cavalry, since they favoured to an unusual degree the use of cavalry in their wars.

For protective devices they used the skins of large snakes, since Libya contains such animals of incredible size, and for offensive weapons, swords and lances; they also used bows and arrows, with which they struck not only when facing the enemy but also when in flight, by shooting backwards at their pursuers with good effect.

Upon entering the land of the Atlantians they defeated in a pitched battle the inhabitants of the city of Cerne, as it is called, and making their way inside the walls along with the fleeing enemy, they got the city into their hands; and desiring to strike terror into the neighbouring peoples they treated the captives savagely, put to the sword the men from the youth upward, led into slavery the children and women, and razed the city.

But when the terrible fate of the inhabitants of Cerne became known among their fellow tribesmen, it is related that the Atlantians, struck with terror, surrendered their cities on terms of capitulation and announced that they would do whatever should be commanded them, and that the Queen Myrina, bearing herself honourably towards the Atlantians, both established friendship with them and founded a city to bear her name in place of the city which had been razed and in it she settled both the captives and any native who so desired whereupon the Atlantians presented her with magnificent presents and by public decree voted to her notable honours, and she in return accepted their courtesy and in addition promised that she would show kindness to their nation.

And since the natives were often being warred upon by the Gorgons, as they were named, a folk which resided upon their borders, and in general had that people lying in wait to injure them, Myrina, they say, was asked by the Atlantians to invade the land of the afore-mentioned Gorgons. But when the Gorgons drew up their forces to resist them a mighty battle took place in which the Amazons, gaining the upper hand, slew great numbers of their opponents and took no fewer than three thousand prisoners

Myrina accorded a funeral to her fallen comrades on three pyres and raised up three great heaps of earth as tombs, which are called to this day Amazon Mounds.

As for Myrina, the account continues, she visited the larger part of Libya, and passing over into Egypt she struck a treaty of friendship with Horus, the son of Isis, who was king of Egypt at that time, and then, after making war to the end upon the Arabians and slaying many of them, she subdued Syria.

She also conquered in war the races in the region of the Taurus, peoples of outstanding courage, and descended through Greater Phrygia to the sea; and then she won over the land lying along the coast and fixed the bounds of her campaign at the Caïcus River (Turkey). And selecting in the territory which she had won by arms sites well suited for the founding of cities, she built a considerable number of them and founded one which bore her own name, but the others she named after the women who held the most important commands, such as Cymê, Pitana, and Prienê.

As mythology relates, their home was on an island which, because it was in the west, was called Hespera, and it lay in the marsh Tritonis. This marsh was near the ocean which surrounds the earth and received its name from a certain river Triton which emptied into it; and this marsh was also near Ethiopia and that mountain by the shore of the ocean which is the highest of those in the vicinity and impinges upon the ocean and is called by the Greeks Atlas.

The island mentioned above was of great size and full of fruit-bearing trees of every kind, from which the natives secured their food. It contained also a multitude of flocks and herds, namely, of goats and sheep, from which possessors received milk and meat for their sustenance; but grain the nation used not at all because the use of this fruit of the earth had not yet been discovered among them.

The Amazons subdued many of the neighbouring Libyans and nomad tribes, and founded within the marsh Tritonis a great city which they named Cherronesus (peninsula) after its shape.

The Amazons attacked Athens, penetrating right to the sacred hill, the acropolis. There the battle reached an awful pitch with Antipode (an Amazon princess who was kidnapped by the Greeks) dying still captive and many other Amazons losing their lives in the heroic, futile effort. The defeated women retreated.

Having subdued many of the neighbouring Lybians and Numidians, they built a city in the lake Tritonis itself.

It is said that an earthquake opening up the parts towards the ocean, and the marsh Tritonides was swallowed up.

The race of these Amazons disappeared entirely many generations before the Trojan War.

As we can see from the detailed accounts of Diodorus it was the Amazons who attacked Greece and an earthquake opened up the earth and swallowed the Amazon city which was in Tritonides.

Greek history is very consistent in supporting the account of Diodorus, but not that of Plato, that it was the Amazons who attacked Greece, not the Atlantians. The Greek historian Priam described the Amazons in battle as ferocious female warriors who were the equal of men and they were greatly admired for their valour. Myrina first attacked the Atlantians in the city of Cerne. This city is described as being an island and city or an island city in some writings. The Greek Historian Polybius also placed Cerne in Mauritania.

In Greek mythology Atlas was a giant Titan who resided in Hyperborea, the sunset island in the west. He was the first king of two separate places: the island of Atlantis (Ireland) and the kingdom of Mauritania, Africa. Over time, the legends of two related places became one. Such is the nature of mythology and ancient history. Truth becomes history, history becomes legend and legend becomes myth, yet the grain of truth endures.

The Eye of the Sahara is a naturally-occurring formation that was utilised by early man for its defensive qualities. Although today it is barren desert at one time it comprised of concentric circles of land and water and connected directly to the Atlantic Ocean by river. Stone Age axes and tools have been found at the site which appear to be of a similar style to those found in Ireland.

There are several legends connecting ancient Ireland to Mauritania. In one Fénius Farsaid and his son Nél, who was married to Scotia - a daughter of an Egyptian pharaoh - travelled from Egypt to Mauritania and on to the pillars of Hercules before sailing to Spain and on to Ireland. The same legend also describes how Fénius Farsaid was one of the 72 chieftains who built the Tower of Babel.

At one time Mauritania was a rich and fertile land dotted with hundreds of lakes and rivers during what is commonly called the African Humid Period when Africa had lots of rainfall. Radar images of the Mauritanian Desert have revealed a vast river network stretching for more than 500km. This formed part of the giant Tamanrasett River which flowed across parts of Western Sahara in ancient times from sources in the southern Atlas Mountains. The river carried water to the sea and water may have coursed through the channels as recently as 5,000 years ago.

People, plants and wildlife would have once thrived in what is now desert. Within a few thousand years, the Sahara went from being rich fertile lands to barren desert. The city of Cerne (Œye of the Sahara) was at one time connected to the sea via a river and surrounded by fresh water. The indigenous people of this region are called the Berbers and are of early Irish descent. Red hair and blue-eyed genetics are found in this region.

The Berbers share many traditions with the Irish, most notably their style of music and language. The traditional Irish *Bodhrán* drum is virtually identical to the *Bendir* drum of the Berbers. Traditional Irish *sean nós* singing is remarkably similar to its Berber equivalent while similarities are also found in the traditional dances of both peoples.

There are unmistakable similarities between the ancient Irish and the Berber language and there are many accounts of native Irish speakers being able to understand the native tongues of Berber tribes due to the similarities of the two languages. The Berbers even play a field sport called *takourt* which is similar to Irish hurling. This sport had been outlawed by French colonists but is still played by youngsters in Morocco today.

The name Berber is derived from the Roman term 'Barbarian', a name they received as they were considered the white race of North Africa. Interestingly, the farming terraces of the Berbers in the Atlas Mountains are virtually identical to those of Machu Picchu in Peru. The Berber Kingdom of Mauritania was at one time an incredibly prosperous kingdom that stretched all across northern Africa. This region is also known as Maghreb which means 'land of the west', 'the land of the Berbers' or 'the land of Atlas'.

The history of the Berber people in northern Africa is extensive and diverse. Archaeologists have traced their origins to the Caspian culture, a North African civilization that dates back more than 10,000 years. Berber-speaking people have lived in North Africa since the earliest times and are first referenced by the Egyptians in 3,000 BC under the name Temehu. Phoenician, Greek, and Roman texts also refer to them.

There is evidence of hundreds of irrigation tunnels in the region which provided the water necessary for producing crops and fruits. Today the structure and surrounding lands are desert however at one time this was a lush fertile pasture abundant in agriculture and exotic wildlife including elephants as described by Plato. Groves of citrus trees produced fruits and many wood tables which were frequently sought out by aristocrats and monarchs.

Further south, the Birimian rocks in nearby Ghana are major sources of gold and diamonds and there are several *disused mines* in the region. Plato described a kingdom with an abundance of gold and ivory. For centuries Ghana has been known as the Gold Coast while its neighbouring country is called the Ivory Coast.

This region is accessible by boat and is probably the location of the legendary lost goldmines of King Solomon.

Visitors to the Eye of the Sahara site have found Stone Age tools, arrowheads and pottery. Seashells, fossils and even whale bones have been found in the area, which is 120m above sea level and 520km from the coast indicating that at one time a large tsunami occurred. Tests on the sand and gravel at the site indicate that the bulk was accumulated sometime between 15,000 and 8,000 years ago, consistent with the date Plato provided for a huge catastrophe around 11,600 years ago.

Evidence has been found in Sudan of a relatively large-scale human armed conflict which occurred around 13,000 years ago. The majority appear to have been killed by archers using flint-tipped arrows and there were two distinct groups, one from southern Africa and one from northern Africa or Europe.

At the centre of this area of Africa is a region of oases. This region is known to the Berber people as Tuat - from the Irish *Tuatha* - meaning 'tribe'. These watering holes are still used today by African tribes when crossing the desert. The Tuat or Touat region is an area in the middle of the Sahara which contains 750,000 date palms in an area of 45sq km. These trees provide edible sweet fruit. What is most remarkable is these trees are nourished by an ancient manmade irrigation system dating back thousands of years. Hundreds of such irrigation systems, which provide water to the driest regions, have been found all over the world. In the Berber region such a manmade system is called a *foggara.* They are also known as a *qanat* in some areas. These water channels were dug using hand tools after underground water channels were found using divining rods. A freshwater spring was also located in the central island of the Eye of the Sahara while irrigation tunnels are found in the nearby plain.

Stone circles and mounds, sometimes called tumuli, are found across the entire world including Africa. In the West African region between the River Gambia and the River Senegal in West Africa alone there are an astonishing 1,053 stone circles and 28,931 monoliths, while stone circles and mounds are found across the entire continent as far south as South Africa. Such constructions are frequently found along coastlines and near rivers.

The Mzoura stone circle in Morocco is particularly important in Berber folklore. Legend claims that this site contains the remains of the giant Antaeus - a key figure in Greek and Berber mythology. Antaeus was known as Anti to the Berbers. Interestingly, Greek-Roman biographer Lucius Plutarch give the following fantastic account of the visit of Roman general Quintus Sertorius to the Kingdom of Mauretania in 82 BC:

In this city the Libyans say that Antaeus is buried; and Sertorius had his tomb dug open, the great size of which made him disbelieve the Barbarians. But when he came upon the body and found it to be sixty cubits long, as they tell us, he was dumbfounded and after performing a sacrifice filled up the tomb again

Sixty cubits is 29m tall - the same size as the biblical Adam according to the Quran. While it's important to treat such a sensational report with a large dose of skepticism, an excavation at the site may well reveal some very interesting findings. Legends of giants are synonymous with both North Africa and Ireland. There is hardly a culture on the planet that doesn't have some myths involving giants. They even make an appearance in the Bible in the famous quote '*there were giants in the earth in those days*' - *Genesis 6:4*

The city of Formia in Italy, which in Roman times was known as Formaie, was said to have been founded by giants. The Fomarie were a giant people who founded settlements in Libya. The Fomorians (*Fomóire* in old Irish) were a race of seafaring giants and the first inhabitants of Ireland. According to the Irish annuals the Fomorians were a seafaring people who never actually arrived in Ireland, they were always there and were said to have been *older than the hills.*

Geoffrey of Monmouth was one of the most renowned scholars ever produced by the island of Britain. According to Geoffrey, the huge stones of Stonehenge were first brought from Africa to Ireland by giants for their healing properties where they were called the 'Giants Ring' or 'Giants Dance' and at a much later date, were forcibly taken to England by Merlin the wizard and Uther Pendragon after slaughtering 7,000 Irish.

Mauritania was a great centre of ancient culture with some regions covered with every type of Stone Age construction imaginable. As many as 10,000, mostly standing stones, have been found in the Mejana Steppe alone. All kinds of megalithic structures are found in the region including stone circles, dolmens, cairns, barrows, and *mounds in the form of step pyramids.* Over thousands of years mounds evolved into step pyramids and eventually pyramids as civilisations developed. The mysterious mound-builders came long before the pyramids.

The history of man in Africa dates back to an incredible antiquity. The world's oldest stone tools have been discovered on the shores of Lake Turkana in Kenya and date back 3.3 million years. They were used by a previously unknown species of pre-humans called *Kenyanthropus platyops.*

Consider that for 3.3 million years primitive man has fumbled around with stone tools until the Stone Age ended around 4,000 years ago. By all scales of evolutionary progress humans should still be far removed from even the most basic understanding of mathematics or language – yet here we are, only 4,000 years later, landing a man on the moon and sending probes deep into space. So, what was the spark for this quantum leap in human intelligence? A mother culture - the sowers of civilisation.

We owe an enormous debt of gratitude to the early sowers of civilisation - the first missionaries who having themselves climbed from the slime of ignorance, travelled the world to push the human race forward. These same people were the first to develop agriculture, invent language and understand mathematics which they used so impressively to build their stone circles and mounds - the temples of the stars found all over the world.

Study the mythologies of the entire world and you will find reference to an early race of *teachers* who arrived sowing the seeds of civilisation. Man is much older than we think.

The true meaning of life is to plant trees under whose shade you do not expect to sit - Nelson Henderson

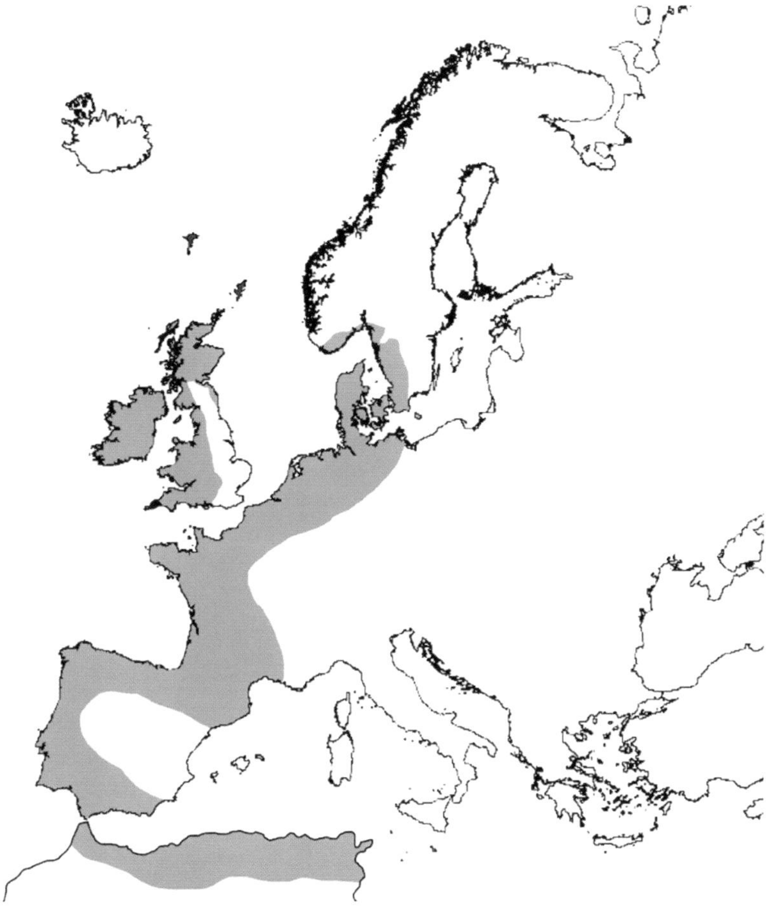

Megalithic map - clearly the builders arrived from the west by sea from Ireland

400,000 years old flint axes found at two separate sites in Ireland. Image - National Museum of Ireland

Stone circle (Asota Sharif Stones) found in Pakistan. Image - Nadeem Faroog Paracha

ASIA

A journey of a thousand miles starts with a single step - Lao Tzu

Stone Age man was a lot more mobile than he has been given credit for and the sea was not the great obstacle it appears to modern man, rather it was the safest and most effective mode of transport until recent history. It has now been proven that Stone Age man sailed to Australia on rafts 65,000 years ago, shattering the previous illusion that Australia has only been occupied for a few centuries, a falsehood promoted by British colonists to hide the mass genocide of the native people, a practice of extermination all too common with colonists.

The pages of human history are soaked in the blood of natives. With a Bible in one hand and a sword in the other, European colonists brought mass murder wherever they went. From the Americas to Australia, Asia to Africa we find colonists reeking in gore as whole generations were butchered and damned. All around the world, these horrific acts led to the European colonists being referred to as *the men without souls.*

The history of native people all across the world has been written by the very colonists who slaughtered them - the men without souls.

The first known humans to arrive in Australia 65,000 years ago encountered giant creatures called megafauna that are now extinct, including enormous birds, 25-foot long lizards, and kangaroos that were five times bigger than today. Islands are the perfect environment for *rapid evolution* and produce more extreme lifeforms which explains why Australia has so many poisonous spiders. Gigantism and dwarfism are particularly common features of island evolution.

There has been a long-standing debate over what could have caused the demise of these giant creatures with some academics arguing that the megafauna extinction was caused by the over hunting of early man, a ridiculous suggestion when you consider the huge numbers of animals, the enormous size of Australia and the primitive tools available to Stone Age man. Is it really likely that early man, armed with a few sharpened stones was capable of slaughtering millions of giant animals? Hardly. Mass extinctions are caused by extreme climate events - such as a mega volcano eruptions or comet impacts which are both capable of creating a huge dust cloud that blocks out the sun's life giving rays which in turn results in a lack of food and mass extinctions.

Maori oral traditions state that upon arrival in New Zealand, the Maori found that there was a large, well-established population already living in the country. The inhabitants were described as having white skin with eye colours from blue to green to darker tints and their hair colour was fair with red being predominant in the general population.

Across New Zealand there are ancient spirals carved into rocks, just like the spirals found in Ireland. The Maori described these first inhabitants as *'Kiri-piwhero'* meaning light-skinned and *'Uru-kehu'* meaning reddish-golden haired. Their modern-day descendants are known as the whaka blonds and display reddish blond hair. This interesting piece is found in Maori legends:

Uru Kehu were the children of Kiwa, the golden ones, the short people with pale freckled skin, blue eyes and fair or red hair.

In some legends these *golden ones* who were described as being light-skinned, red-haired *people of peace* came via the sea from Peru while in other legends the ancient *golden ones* came to New Zealand from Easter Island or from the Tarim Basin in China where hundreds of red-haired mummies have been found.

The 'Beauty of Loulan' is the most famous of the Tarim mummies. She has reddish-brown hair and white skin. Several other mummies found in the region have red hair including 'Cherchen Man' who, like the rest of the Tarim Mummies, is famous for European-like facial features and clothing. Cherchen Man stands like an old Celtic warrior with reddish-brown hair, pale skin and a ginger beard. He's every inch a Celt and even his DNA says so. Genetic testing confirms that he and hundreds of other mummies found in Xinjiang's Tarim Basin contain European DNA. The wooden combs they used are familiar to students of ancient Celtic art, while the burial sites of Cherchen Man and his fellow people were marked with stone structures similar to Irish dolmens and standing stones.

These finds are forcing academics to re-examine old Chinese books that describe historical figures of great height, with blue or green eyes, long noses, full beards, and red or blond hair. Academics had ridiculed these accounts in the past, but it now seems that they are accurate.

Dolmens are also found across the four corners of the world in Asia, Europe, Africa and America. The word dolmen means *stone table*. Dolmens are also called portal tombs, passage tombs or giant's tables. Some of the capstones weigh an extraordinary amount. The heaviest capstone on earth weighs an astonishing 100 tons and is found on the Brownshill dolmen in County Carlow, Ireland.

A huge quantity of dolmens are found in India, while the largest concentration of dolmens in the entire world is found on the Korean Peninsula. With an estimated 35,000 dolmens, Korea alone accounts for nearly 40% of the world's total. Some of the capstones on these dolmens are of enormous size.

The Middle East also had a huge quantity of dolmens, cairns and stone circles in ancient times and the divided people of this region have an ancient shared history that could help unite them as does the entire world. Dolmens and standing stones have been found in large areas of the Middle East. They can be found in Turkey, Syria, Yemen, Lebanon, Syria, Iran, Israel, Jordan, and Saudi Arabia.

Megaliths have also been found in Iran and Iraq. Karahunge is a site in Armenia consisting of 223 individual stones of which only 37 are still standing. Some of these weigh up to 10 tons and around a third have circular holes drilled in them.

An underwater stone circle was found at Atlit Yam in Israel. As the site is now submerged under the sea it has earned it the nickname 'Israel's Atlantis'. It is around 9,000 years old making it a very early example of stone circles in the region. Atlit Yam is located close to several key biblical locations - its 155km to Bethlehem, 150km to Jerusalem and less than 50km to Nazareth. Hundreds of standing stones have been found in the region. The Druids worshipped in groves and erected standing stone pillars. Both make an appearance in the Bible:

And Abraham planted a grove - Genesis 21:33

Moses got up early the next morning and built an altar at the foot of the mountain and set up twelve stone pillars - Exodus 24:4

And Joshua set up at Gilgal the twelve stones they had taken out of the Jordan - Joshua 4:20

The term *Gilgal,* which means a *circle of stones* is mentioned 39 times in the Hebrew Bible.

The original name of the biblical figure Abraham was actually Abram. This is remarkably similar to Abhras, the Irish Druid who taught Pythagoras and was described by the Greeks as being a great healer, teacher and prophet.

During the Dark Ages, it was widely believed that standing stones were built by the giants who lived before the biblical flood. Many were destroyed or defaced by early Christians; it is estimated that in

Europe alone some 50,000 megaliths were destroyed, and countless ancient texts and temples were burned.

The ancient Irish language is remarkably similar to ancient Hebrew, Chaldean, Arabic and Sanskrit, proving a direct relationship between these regions from the earliest of times. Language is the great proof of the origin of nations - those with the same language had the same origin. Language is a living history. The close resemblance between Irish Gaelic and many of the Asiatic tongues is conclusive proof that old Irish Gaelic is one of the oldest languages on earth, if not the oldest.

All the languages of the western world were the same, and that one system of letters, that of ancient Irish Druids, pervaded the whole - and was common to the British Isles, and Gaul, to the inhabitants of Italy, Greece, Syria, Arabia, Persia, and Hindoostan - Godfrey Higgins, Celtic Druids

That the ancient Irish had an alphabet is evident from the many similarities that are only found in other ancient languages. It is astonishing to think that the propaganda of the Dark Ages, designed to tarnish Ireland's reputation, still persists in academic circles today, as they blindly insist that the Irish ogham alphabet wasn't invented until the fifth century. However, ogham writing was found on the Shigar idol in Russia which has been dated as 11,500 years old. Presumably when the Irish invented ogham in the fifth century they also invented a time machine.

Edmund Spencer is considered one of the greatest ever English poets and his poem *The Faerie Queen* is regarded as a masterpiece. Spencer was no friend of the Irish - he campaigned vigorously for the complete destruction of the Irish language, the elimination of the Brehon laws and the *extermination of the natives by famine*. He did however confirm the antiquity of the Irish alphabet in his writings:

For when you say the Irish have always been without letters, you are therein much deceived ; For it is certain, that Ireland hath had the use of letters very anciently, and long before England- Edmund Spencer

Several scholars have claimed that Ireland is the *Golden Island* mentioned in Sanskrit texts. Ignatius Donnelly, the US senator who single-handedly kept the legend of Atlantis alive, had this to say about Ireland:

There are many evidences that the old world recognised Ireland as possessing a very ancient civilization. In the Sanskrit books it is referred to as Hiranya, the 'Island of the Sun', to wit, of sun-worship; in other words, as pre-eminently the centre of that religion which was shared by all the ancient races of Europe, Asia, Africa, and America. It is believed that Ireland was the 'Garden of Phoebus' (Hyperborea) of the Western mythologists - Ignatius Donnelly, Atlantis: the Antediluvian World

General Charles Vallancey was a British military surveyor sent to Ireland in 1770 to assist in a military survey of the island, which he made his adopted home. He became an expert in Irish history and wrote several books on the subject which demonstrated the remarkable link between the old Irish language and several other ancient tongues. Vallancey and some other notable scholars proposed that Ireland was *Suvarna-dwip (the Golden Island)* while Britain was *Sueta-dwip (the White Island)* found in the *Brahmanda Purana* Sanskrit texts and there is some evidence to support this claim.

According to certain Sanskrit texts, the *Maga* were Brahmins who came from an island in the west. In old Irish *Magh* means Druid while the *Magi* were the priests of ancient Iran. In Brahmin circles there was a belief in a remote western island of Maga who followed the Brahmanical order of society.

In one legend, three Hindu deities travelled to Svetadvipa on a *chariot of swans* where the inhabitants of that island had *complexions as white as the rays of the moon.*

Some scholars have made the east to west link between ancient Ireland and India however, few have considered the possibility of a *west to east* migration despite the pattern of coastal and river settlements around the world strongly suggesting an Atlantic origin. The Indians were not a seafaring people and have never sent out colonies for exploration however there is an abundance of evidence for migrations from Ireland.

How could the Sanskrit writings have preserved maps of Ireland, England, and Spain, giving the shape and outline of their coasts and their very names, and yet have preserved no memory of the expeditions or colonisations by which they acquired that knowledge?
- Ignatius Donnelly, Atlantis: the Antediluvian World

There are a lot of similarities between Indian and Irish culture and its clear they have been connected from ancient times. The ancient Irish Brehon laws have only one equivalent on earth - the Sanskrit laws. Many musical instruments found in India have their roots in Ireland while the seven-syllable verse used in Old Irish has the same origin as that of the Indian Rig Veda. The seafaring nature of the Irish explains why no other western European culture has such similarities - they were in contact from the earliest of times.

Apart from the dramatic similarities of the languages one of the most striking similarities is in astronomy. Both the Druids and the Brahman had knowledge of the precession of the equinox, a 25,920-year astronomical cycle known as the Great Year.

How long does a civilisation need to be observing the stars to develop such advanced knowledge?

The ancient Irish and Hindus both used the name 'Budh' for the planet Mercury. The stem *budh* appears in all the Celtic languages, as it does in Sanskrit, and means 'all victorious,' 'gift of teaching,' 'accomplished,' 'enlightened,' 'exalted' and so on. A Budha or Buddha was a wise teacher or one who has reached enlightenment, wisdom - a golden *unreactive* mind that has conquered the passionate lower animal mind and is neither a positive or negative thinker - it is a perfect balance of both.

The Greek messenger god Hermes is also associated with the planet Mercury. As the planet Mercury is closer to the sun than earth it was considered more spiritually evolved as it is *closer to the light of the world*, the sun. The ancients honoured nature and its great emblem - the sun - the source of all life on this planet.

The similarities of teachings demonstrate the common heritage of the Druid and Brahmin. The scientific religion of the Druids was a system of philosophy and the rich mother soil out of which all of the world's religions and civilisations grew. The word philosophy means the '*love of wisdom*'.

Honour was the aim of the Druid and they valued wisdom and virtue above all else. They had a scientific religion and worshipped nature and its great emblems - the sun, the moon and the earth. Their chief object of adoration was the sun - the light of the world.

In Sanskrit, *arya* means *freeman,* and in old Irish *aire* means *nobleman.* The term *arya* is frequently used in Buddhist texts to designate a spiritual warrior or hero, not a race of people. The word Aryan may have been derived from the word *Éireann* - Ireland's ancient name - which is pronounced Eir-e-ann. The term Aryan has been completely misused and hijacked by numerous groups, most notably the Nazis and modern-day white supremacists.

For the record there is no master race and never was, there is only the human race and a thousand generations live in all of us.

The Babylonians were a spectacular ancient civilisation based in modern day Iran, Iraq, Syria, Kuwait, Turkey. Of all their legendary achievements they are best remembered for the Hanging Gardens of Babylon, also known as the Hanging Gardens of Semiramis which was said to have been a truly incredible structure and one of the Seven Wonders of the Ancient World, the only one yet to be found.

While some argue that the gardens were a work of fiction, this explanation lacks credibility as there are several independent, yet similar, accounts of its existence from important historians including Diodorus, Strabo and Quintus. These accounts contain similarities including tiered gardens, canals, a nearby river and *water-raising screws.*

The most widely-held view is that the gardens were constructed by King Nebuchadnezzar II however, this is not accurate. He constructed a fabulous palace known as 'the marvel of mankind' however this was not the Hanging Gardens - it was a separate palace in a separate region.

The Hanging Gardens were actually constructed by the Assyrian king Sennacherib for his palace at Nineveh. Over the centuries stories of the two palaces became confused. In several legends, the hanging gardens were said to have been built to remind the homesick queen of the green hills and valleys of her homeland.

The remains of the Hanging Gardens of Babylon are located in Mosul in modern-day Iraq near the river Tigris.

Archaeological excavations have found traces of a vast system of aqueducts attributed to Sennacherib by an inscription on its remains. This was part of a series of canals, dams, and aqueducts used to carry water to Nineveh with *water-raising screws* used to raise water to the upper levels of the gardens. Sennacherib called his new palace and garden a 'wonder for all peoples' and described the making and operation of screws to raise water in his garden.

The following is part of a notice which appeared in the *Magazine Encyclopedique*, printed in Paris in 1800.

Cabinet of Antiquities of the National Library.

Permit me, through the means of your journal, to make known to the lovers of Chaldean Antiquities a precious monument, which I have bought from Persia.

It is a stone of the nature of basalt, eighteen inches high and twelve broad, weighing forty-four pounds.

The surface is entirely covered with inscriptions. The letters or characters are formed of straight strokes, without any rounding or turning, as we see in the characters of other languages.

I found it about a day's journey from Bagdad, in the ruins of a palace called the Garden of Semiramis, near the river Tigris. The ruins show it was once a very magnificent palace; there are immense subterraneans and aqueducts.

It is very probable that the people of the interior of Persia, and those who inhabited the banks of the Tigris and Euphrates, at the time this monument was inscribed, had the same language.

This discovery was made by a Frenchman named Monsieur Michaux. Here we have confirmation that the Garden of Semiramis is located near the river Tigris and that Irish ogham writing, the only known alphabet to consist of *straight strokes* was found in the famous garden. Perhaps the homesick queen missed the green hills and valleys of her homeland in the Emerald Isle.

There are links between ancient Iran and Ireland going back to the very dawn of civilisation. *Anu* was the supreme god of the Ancient Babylonians and supreme goddess of the Ancient Irish. The Babylonian Anunnaki and the Irish Tuatha Dé Danann are both named after Anu.

The Magi were the priests of Mesopotamia. In the ancient Irish annals, the word *magh* was sometimes used as an alternative to the word *draoi*, a Druid. The Magi roots lead back to the Druids.

The Prophet Zoroaster was the founder of the Magi priesthood and his teachings became the dominant religion in Ancient Persia - a spectacular kingdom that stretches back to 7,000 BC, long before the rise of Ancient Egypt, Greece or Rome.

Where exactly Zoroaster came from or when exactly he lived remains a complete mystery that has baffled scholars for centuries. All that is known about Zoroaster is that he lived at least one thousand years before the Bible was compiled, if not much earlier, leading many prominent scholars to conclude that the ancient myths of the Persians were repackaged by the authors of the Bible.

In 'The Origin of All Religious Worship' (1872) by Charles-François Dupuis, a French professor at the Collège de Lisieux in Paris we find this intriguing reference to Zoroaster and 'Eiren'. While 'Eiren' has been interpreted by some to mean Iran, Éirinn is Ireland's ancient name.

The God of Light and of the good principle, informs Zoroaster, that he had given to man a place of delight and abundance.... this place was called 'Eiren', which at the beginning was more beautiful than all the World... Nothing could equal the beauty of this delightful place....

Instead of Eiren, the Hebrew copyists have put Eden, as the two letters, 'r' and 'd' in that language, have a remarkable resemblance...

It is principally the religion of the Magi, from which that of the Christians is derived. We shall not look therefore for anything in the Genesis of the Hebrews, which we shall not find in that of the Magi.

The reader is reminded that the biblical 'three wise men' were Magi astrologers. Several authors have made the connection between the Irish Druids and the Persian Magi including Henry O'Brien, author of 'The Round Towers of Ireland' who also claimed that Ireland's mysterious round towers were pre-Christian Druid towers.

It's worth noting that Charles Vallancey in his 'Vindication of the Ancient History of Ireland' (1786) claimed that Zoroaster was none other than Nuada Airgetlám - Nuada of the Silver Hand - a member of Ireland's 'Tribe of the Gods' - the Tuatha Dé Danann. In 'Phoenician Ireland' by Henry O'Brien we are also informed that the actual silver hand of Nuada, a priceless historical artefact was last seen in storage at the London 'Society of Antiquaries'. Several enquiries made to the society by the author as to the whereabouts of this incredible artefact have not been responded to.

At one time Iran was known as the *sacred land* and Ireland as the *sacred island.* Ireland is famous for a three-leafed plant called the shamrock. In the Arabic world a three-leafed plant or trefoil shape is called a *shamrak.*

The Gobekli Tepe complex in Turkey is around 11,000 years old and is without doubt one of the most important historical sites on earth. It is a truly remarkable discovery of enormous historical significance. The incredible stone carvings, astronomical alignments and overall complexity of the site are obvious indicators that this was not the first temple ever built - the advanced architectural and construction skills needed to create such a masterpiece were many thousands of years in development. Such structures are built on previous knowledge, the skills needed to build them are refined over hundreds of generations.

Work at the site started around 11,000 years ago - shortly after the end of the Younger Dryas mini Ice Age period, a time of extraordinary global upheaval. Stone carvings from the site depict a devastating comet impact around the time of the Younger Dryas mini Ice Age period and the author suggests a huge comet impact in the Atlantic ocean triggered a tsunami, that drowned Atlantis Ireland and resulted in a huge period of global flooding and rainfall - the 'great deluge' found in virtually all the world's cultures. In science this flooding event is called Meltwater Pulse 1B.

It seems as though the advanced builders of Gobekli Tepe appeared out of nowhere bringing with them advanced skills which they used to build their star temple - an advanced type of stone circle.

Overenthusiastic journalists often claim Gobekli Tepe is the world's oldest temple. This is clearly not the case, it's much too advanced, earlier temples were much simpler and more primitive. The earliest temples were groves, standing stones, cairns and mounds.

The dawning of a new civilisation marks the twilight of an old one. The Fertile Crescent was the birthplace of a new civilisation. Its mother was an old one - the Mound Builders.

When you witness the majesty of Ireland's mounds, the fertility of her soil, and the poetry of her people you get the sense that this is the place where time itself first began.

A wise man makes his own decisions.

An ignorant man follows public opinion

- Chinese Proverb

Gochang Dolmen in South Korea is identical in style to Irish dolmens

Dolmen found in Gamla Nature Reserve, Golan Heights - 76km from Nazareth, Israel

AMERICA

Only when the last tree has been cut and the last river poisoned will man realise that you can't eat money.
- Native American Proverb

The mounds of America are the same as the mounds of Ireland because the same people built them. Man sailed for thousands of years before he first saddled a horse and the sea was not the great obstacle it appears today, rather it was the safest and most effective mode of transport from the Stone Age right up until the invention of the steam engine.

The scientific name for our species is *Homo sapiens* which in Latin means 'wise man'. The size and functionality of the human brain compared to other species is what makes humans so unique. As a result of these big brains, humans are excellent problem solvers, great toolmakers and are highly adaptable to changing environments. Humans are also very arrogant.

Modern man greatly overestimates his own intelligence and underestimates the intelligence of his ancestors.

That big brain has been walking around earth for at least 200,000 years if not much longer. How long do you think it took early man to realise that wood floats? The earliest boats were simple constructions - log-boats, paddle-boards and rafts made from wood held together with cord.

Since man sailed to Australia 65,000 years ago on rafts, it's logical to suggest he also reached America by the same method. Dozens of sites dating back tens of thousands of years have been found all along the American coastline. These sites are found on both sides of the continent, from Alaska to Chile on the west coast and from Brazil to Pennsylvania on the east coast, strongly suggesting a *coastal migration.*

Humans have been on the American continent for much longer than current estimates. Evidence of human life at the Bluefish Caves in Canada dates back 24,000 years while two sites, one in South Carolina and one in Brazil have produced carbon-datings that indicate human life 50,000 - 60,000 years ago however, these dates have proven controversial and have not yet been accepted by mainstream academics.

Mounds are found all over the world. They are the seed out of which grew all the great pyramid structures found in South America, Egypt, Iraq, China and several other countries. The first mounds were a small pile of stones covered with earth. As civilisation evolved, ever-larger mounds were constructed usually in circular shapes, although there were variations. Some were pyramid-shaped, others had platforms like step pyramids while others were shaped like various different creatures, the most famous of which is the Great Serpent Mound in Ohio, USA. This huge structure is built on the crater of a cosmic impact that occurred millions of years ago. A serpent mound is also found on the other side of the Atlantic at Lochnell, Scotland.

While mounds were the ancestors of pyramids, cairns were the ancestors of mounds. Cairns came first. A *cairn* is an Irish word which means a man-made pile of rocks and was the first form of construction due to its absolute simplicity. The first builders gathered stones and created small piles of rocks to mark gravestones, signposts, landmarks and as early temples. Ancestor worship was practiced by early man and the more important the person, the larger the cairn. Cairns developed into ever-larger structures of various shapes, usually circular, and ranged from small rock sculptures to huge man-made hills of stone.

Over time cairns evolved into mounds. The difference between the two is a cairn is a stone-only construction while a mound is an earthwork of both stone and soil. A cairn is a man-made pile of stone while a mound is a man-made hill. The oldest mounds were piles of stones topped with a layer of earth just like icing on a cake. Various cultures all around the world still erect cairns and mounds today.

Cairns, mounds, standing stones, dolmens and stone circles are all forms of megaliths and are found on every continent on earth. Stone circles have been found all across the Americas including in the USA, Canada, Mexico, Peru, Columbia, Brazil, Argentina, Chile and the Caribbean. A giant dolmen found at North Salem, New York has a capstone estimated to weigh an incredible 90 tons.

In North America cairns and mounds are both associated with the native American people and are found across the entire American continent from Alaska to the Andes. An *inuksui* is a form of cairn - they are stacked rocks used as a landmark that are found all over the artic region of Canada, Greenland and Alaska. Rock cairns were also used to mark buffalo driving lanes at Native American sites that date back as much as 12,000 years.

There are many similarities between the cultures of old America and old Ireland that simply cannot be explained by modern contact, these similarities go right back to the most ancient of times.

The Algonquian is a collective name for a huge group of native American tribes and their languages. Historically, these people were prominent along the Atlantic Coast and their language bears a remarkable resemblance to old Irish Gaelic. In fact, not only is there huge similarities, many words are virtually identical. Language is living history and those with the same language had the same origin.

The Duhare tribe in South Carolina and Georgia had white skin, red hair, freckles and were noticeably taller than other natives in the area. Their leaders had beards and they domesticated deer like cattle - these deer were butchered for meat while their milk was used to make cheese. While milking a deer may seem strange, it's well-known that several Irish tribes had domesticated deer and deer milk has been celebrated in Gaelic poetry. We find the following reference to deer milk in an ancient Irish lullaby entitled *Bainne nam fiadh:*

On milk of deer I was reared. On milk of deer I was nurtured.

The word Duhare can be translated as *du'hEir*, meaning 'place of the Irish.' When native American researchers investigated the connections between Duhare and Irish Gaelic they found stunning similarities. For example, the word *fia* means deer in both languages. Rock carvings similar to those found in Ireland are also found in South Carolina. The Duhare people were not the only tall red-haired natives in America, as other similar tribes have been observed across the continent. The Mandan tribe of North and South Dakota told early French explorers that there were natives in the region that had fair skin with red or blonde hair and blue eyes. The Paiute tribe of Nevada have long spoken of red-haired giants known as the Si-Te-Cah while legends from Midwestern tribes tell of yellow-or-red haired giants living around the Great Lakes.

Red-haired mummies have been found all across North America in Michigan, Illinois, New York, Virginia, Arizona, and Nevada. The Chinchorro mummies are a set of mummies found in Northern Chile. They are the oldest mummies in the world, the oldest is an incredible 7,400 years old. Several of the mummies have reddish auburn hair and genetic testing confirms they contain European DNA. The mysterious Paracas mummies of Peru have red-hair and strange elongated skulls.

There are Spanish records from the 1500s describing several red-haired native American tribes which seemed so absurd to academics that they have been ignored for centuries. Some scholars have speculated that due to the similarities of language, customs and appearance, the Irish arrived hundreds of years before Columbus. This is only partly true - they arrived *thousands* of years beforehand.

Names written on ogham stones in Ireland such as Winter Wolf, Black Raven and Little Badger are identical to the style of names used by native American tribes. Irish ogham writing has been found all across North America.

Dr. Barry Fell, a Harvard University professor, found ogham writing on rocks all across America including sites in West Virginia, California, Connecticut, Nevada, Oklahoma, Kansas and Vermont USA as well as Canadian sites in Alberta and British Columbia. His 1976 book, *America BC,* which includes photographs of these finds, proved highly controversial upon its release and remains so today. Independent to Fell's work ogham has also been found at several other US sites. Rock dust that had caked over the ogham writing at one site provided a carbon-dating of 1,000 BC while another ogham site depicted an astronomical event that occurred in 471 AD.

The mounds of America have been associated with giants for centuries. Native American legends tell of a giant race of *mound-builders* called the Alligewi. The Allegheny River and Mountains are named after these people who were said to have been the remnants of a once numerous and highly civilised people. These mysterious giants were said to have ranged between *seven and ten feet tall* and were buried beneath America's mounds. Even United States President Abraham Lincoln made reference to *'the giants whose bones fill the mounds of America'*.

A *New York Times* article from 1897 described a mound in Wisconsin in which a giant human skeleton measuring over 9ft (2.7m) in length was found. Another *New York Times* article from 1886 described gigantic human thigh bones found at a mound in Cartersville, Georgia. Based on the size of these thigh bones the height of their owners was estimated at 14ft. Robert Wadlow was born and raised in Alton, Illinois, USA. He died in 1940 having reached the astonishing height of 8ft 11in. All around the world we find numerous legends of an early race of red-haired giants (7-10ft tall). In Greek mythology, the kings of Hyperborea were said to be 10ft tall.

Gigantism and dwarfism are not genetic mutations - they are genetic memories - expressions of our ancient past.

Gigantism is caused by the AIP gene and the highest concentration in the entire world of this 'giant gene' is found in Mid-Ulster, Ireland where 1 in 150 people carry this DNA.

In South America we find numerous references to a white-skinned red-haired race. According to local legends these *teachers* arrived in boats sowing the seeds of civilisation. They taught the natives how to domesticate animals, grow crops and create rich fertile soil using charcoal, a technique called *Terra Preta* that is still used today in the Amazon. They also taught them construction and hunting techniques and how to understand the movements of the sun and moon to predict the seasons. At that time early man was primitive and had little knowledge of how the seasons worked or how to grow crops.

Over time these early advanced people became god men in the legends of natives because of their knowledge and their strange appearance. They were taller, pale skinned and had a hair colour just like the sun, piercing blue eyes and red beards - all of which would have seemed alien to the natives. These people were Irish Druids who, having sown the seeds of civilisation in a particular area, left in their boats to continue their mission. Having seen the sorry state of their fellow man these early missionaries left their home in the sunset land of Ireland not to build an empire but to push the human race forward. Some stayed and formed settlements. Humans are tribal by nature. Study human history and you will observe that the most respected member of a tribe was not the warrior, hunter or leader - it was the wise teacher.

In South America we find enormous similarities with ancient Irish culture. The construction style of Machu Picchu is almost identical to the Irish monastery in Skellig Michael. Mounds, stone circles and megaliths are found all over the entire south American continent. Ireland's great hero Cú Chulainn is similar in name to the

Maya god-king Kukulkan. One of the finest temples in all of South American is called the Temple of Kukulkan.

The transatlantic slave trade was born in the Vatican in 1452 when Pope Nicholas V issued a papal bull called *Dum Diversas* which gave the King of Portugal full permission to conquer overseas lands and enslave the natives. Three years later he issued another bull called *Romanus Pontifex* confirming this right to conquest and enslave. Similar bulls were issued by several other Popes including Pope Callixtus III (*Inter Caetera Quae,* 1456), Pope Sixtus IV (*Aeterni Regis,* 1481), and Pope Leo X (*Precelse Denotionis,* 1514).

In 1488, Pope Innocent VIII (who fathered a number of illegitimate children), happily accepted a gift of 100 black slaves which were distributed among his favourite bishops.

After Christopher Columbus had rediscovered the Americas, the Spanish king asked Pope Alexander VI to confirm Spain's ownership of these newly-found lands and in 1493 he issued the *Bulls of Donation,* three papal bulls called *Inter Caetera*, *Eximiae Devotionis,* and *Dudum Siquidem* which granted Spain the rights to these overseas territories.

When the Spanish Conquistadors first arrived in South America the natives believed it was the return of the friendly god-men to their shores once more. How wrong they were. They could not imagine, not even in the darkest corners of their minds, the mayhem and destruction that these strangers were about to inflict upon them and their world. With a Bible in one hand and a sword in the other the Spanish proceeded to unleash mayhem on the natives who had welcomed them with open arms. It was nothing short of a bloodbath. Shiploads of gold and silver were sent back to the colonists of Spain and the Vatican who built palaces with the proceeds. Those who didn't die by the sword died of European diseases like smallpox, from which they had no immunity.

Millions of indigenous people died as the result of European colonists actions all across the Americas. Books were burned, civilisations destroyed and temples ransacked. The deceptions of the colonists - that America was virtually uninhabited before their arrival and that most natives died of naturally occurring diseases - endures to this day. Spineless historians refuse to discuss the horrific ethnic cleansing that ravished the great continent. The colonial powers told the world they brought civilisation to barbaric natives. The truth is they brought pillage, genocide and slavery as they became known to the natives as *the men without souls*.

The lessons of the past are to be forgiven but not forgotten. Those who fail to learn from the mistakes of history are doomed to repeat them while those who fail to even question history itself are pitiful creatures. The current mainstream version of history is a house of cards that's about to come crashing down and there are many great historical treasures yet to be discovered in the Americas.

The native Americans have many fabulous tales and moral stories which contain great wisdom. The indigenous Ojibwe people of north-eastern America have told the *king of the birds* story for generations. The tale describes how all the birds were arguing over which one was the king of the birds, and it was decided that whichever bird could fly the highest was indeed the king. The tiny wren jumped on to the back of the mighty eagle who soared higher than all the other birds and when the eagle could go no higher the tiny wren flew off his back to an even greater height and that was how the little wren became the king of the birds. The exact same story has been told to Irish children for thousands of years.

Native people all around the world used stories to give hope and teach wisdom. They learned the hard way that it's not those who can inflict the most suffering, but those who can endure it who eventually prevail.

The land of opportunity spawned a whole new breed of men without souls

- Don Henley

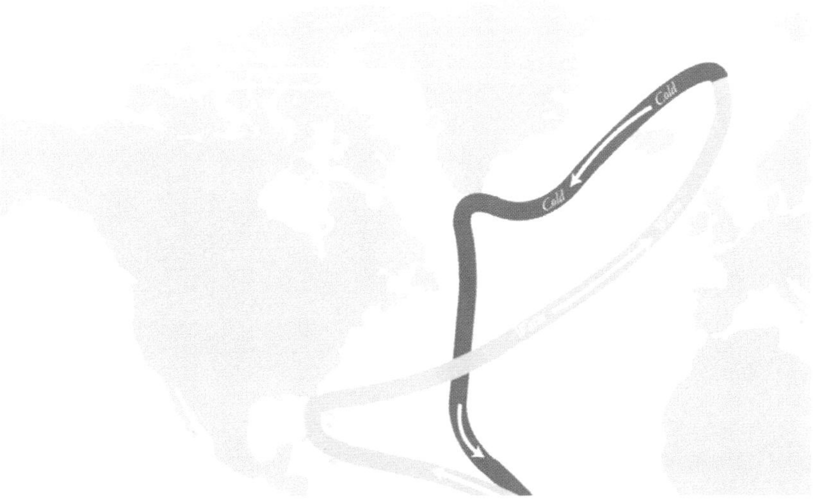

The warm Atlantic Gulf Stream did not stop during the the Ice Age

The Atlantian Irish sailed to Iceland then Greenland before reaching the Americas

Irish ogham writing on the Blanchard Stone, Vermont, USA

Rock carvings on the Reinhardt Boulder, Georgia USA are identical to those found on Irish stones

EUROPE

The ancient Romans built their greatest masterpieces of architecture, their amphitheaters, for wild beasts to fight in
- Voltaire

The Celts didn't come to Ireland, they came *from* Ireland. What is so blatantly obvious to the layperson is labelled 'pseudoscience' by academics who can't see what's right under their noses. Common sense is not that common, especially in the ivory towers of academia.

When the Stone Age Irish built Newgrange they used boats capable of transporting 10-ton boulders. A boat capable of such a feat was a remarkable piece of engineering and easily able to handle the high seas. Modern man, with all his technology and tools would struggle to move such a huge weight. During the building of Newgrange, 97 huge boulders were transported by boat from Clogherhead beach which is 30km away. All this proves that the ancient Irish had superb boats long before the pyramids were built, and the advanced knowledge required to build such a boat was many thousands of years in development.

Just like bees swarm from a hive, the Atlantian Irish sailed from their sacred island to set up home on pastures new. The megalithic mother culture sailed from Ireland and a simple glance at any megalithic map of Europe makes it obvious that the builders arrived by sea. The high concentration of megaliths on the west cost of Britain and France proves that Ireland was the fountainhead, the source of the *megalithic mother culture.*

Stone circles and megalithic constructions are found on the remote islands in the north Atlantic including the Orkney, Shetland, and Faroe Islands. Take, for example, the remote Faroe Islands which are approximately halfway between Ireland and Iceland in the North

Atlantic Ocean. The official history of the Faroes is that these small remote islands were uninhabited before the first Vikings arrived in the 9th century AD. However, archaeologists have found definitive proof that people were living on the Faroe Islands centuries beforehand. These people grew barley, burned peat and erected standing stones. This is yet more proof of a megalithic seafaring people in the Atlantic Ocean long before the Vikings.

When the Vikings first arrived in nearby Iceland, they found that the Irish had already been there. Stone circles that were built long before then Vikings have been found all over Scandinavia. The only logical explanation is that the builders of these megaliths arrived much earlier by boat - a *megalithic mother culture.*

The understanding of human history will take a quantum leap forward once academics realise man has been sailing for tens of thousands of years. The Atlantian Irish started sailing the high seas during the Stone Age and never stopped. They mingled with other cultures and left their mark and their genetics.

The megalithic mother culture used the Faroe Islands, Iceland and Greenland as steeping stones to reach America and the stone circles found in all these locations prove this claim. The megalithic builders left the fountainhead of Ireland and created settlements all over the world. Some were missionaries who sowed the seeds of civilisation. Others were settlers who sought new lands. Others were fugitives. In old Ireland the ultimate penalty was not death - it was exile.

Today the term Celts is used to describe a loose collection of people all over Europe. Modern-day Ireland, Scotland, Wales, Cornwall (England) and Brittany (France) were particular strongholds of Celtic culture. The Celts have been portrayed as lawless barbarians by the Romans and Greeks. It should be remembered that the *Senones*, a French tribe led by a chieftain named Brennus defeated the Romans at the Battle of thc Allia in 390 BC. Three years later, in 387 BC, he led an army of Italian Celts in their attack on Rome where they captured the city, holding it for several months. Brennus' sack of Rome was the only time in 800 years the city was occupied by a non-Roman army. Seeing their city devastated, the Romans attempted to buy their salvation from Brennus and agreed to pay one thousand pounds weight of gold for him and his army to leave. These events left a deep scar on the Roman psyche and go a long way to explaining their hatred for the Celts and destruction of its civilisation. After the Roman invasion of Britain, the English largely disowned its ancient history because it came from Ireland - the older brother it grew to despise.

Cro-Magnon man is thought to have been the first modern human (*Homo sapiens*) who lived in Europe from at least 50,000 years ago. They received the name Cro-Magnon because their skeletons were first discovered in a cave in Cro-Magnon, France in 1868. Fossil remains have been found all over Europe from Bulgaria to Britain. These people were intelligent hunters who used spears and javelins to hunt large animals. They were also advanced enough to speak a primitive language, make early musical instruments and draw cave paintings.

The Cro-Magnons (also known as Early European Modern Man or EEMA) made a strong cord which was used to tie together stone tools, weave baskets and bind primitive clothes. Cord and wood is all you need to build a Stone Age boat and the skill needed to make a spear is the same skill needed to make a boat. To make either, you need to be able to shape the wood and tie it together with cord. A primitive musical whistle was found in a site in Germany, while beautiful cave art was found in France. This proves these people were not mindless cavemen as they are often portrayed. Our ancestors were a lot smarter than they have been given credit for and it seems that early human civilisation made huge progress in Europe during this time.

For a long time, Cro-Magnon man was considered a *separate species* to modern *Homo sapiens* however, it is now considered the same species. The Cro-Magnons had a well-built body, a short broad face and they were relatively tall - the tallest skeleton found was 6ft 3in tall.

The Cro Magnons had one other very significant characteristic - they had huge brains, 20% larger than today's humans.

Not only were our ancestors smarter than we have given them credit for but they also had giant brains.

Scientists have been unable to explain why the size of human brains has been shrinking for the last 10,000 years.

When the Canary Islands were first discovered by the Spaniards early in the 15th century they found a native people called the Guanches who had blue eyes and reddish blond hair. The Guanches are thought to have been Cro-Magnons who were genetically isolated for thousands of years and several red-haired mummies were preserved. DNA testing of the mummies confirms that the Guanches share an ancestry with a people that science calls the *Atlantic Europeans.*

They also share an ancestry with the Berbers of North Africa and the Basques of the Pyrenees, who both share an ancestry with the *Atlantic Europeans.* Science has now proven that men with the genetic Haplogroup R1b are *direct descendants* of the Cro-Magnons.

Ireland and Wales have the highest concentration of R1b on Earth. In some parts of Ireland 95% of all males carry this gene.

Despite the size of their huge brains, the mysterious Cro-Magnons have largely been overlooked by science. Speculation regarding our big-brained ancestors has largely been ridiculed as 'pseudoscience' - the scientific equivalent of blasphemy - a term reserved for those who dare question the official dogma as decreed by the high priests of academia. Today there is as much dogma in science as religion.

Islands are natural laboratories and the perfect environment for evolution. A limited gene-pool, a lack of predators and sharp boundaries all create unique evolutionary pressures which often trigger dramatic changes such as gigantism and dwarfism. This pattern is found in islands all over the world and the fossil record suggests that *evolutionary changes can occur rapidly* after a species has become isolated on an island - much faster than on a mainland. A species isolated on a remote island can undergo *accelerated evolution* in a relatively short space of time - between a few decades and several thousand years. In other words, they can take an *evolutionary quantum leap.*

Evolution is not limited to a slow gradual process. *Quantum leaps can and do occur* in relatively short spaces of time and the most extreme evolutionary changes are found on the smallest, most remote *ocean* islands.

Modern man is a *quantum leap* in evolution that science cannot fully explain. Both the 'Out of Africa' theory of evolution and the 'East to West' theory of human migrations are incomplete. A big piece of human history - the keystone - is missing. The author offers a highly controversial theory that deserves scientific investigation.

Cro-Magnon man (Homo Sapiens) first evolved in Ireland after an earlier human species (Homo Antecessor) got isolated there in the very distant past.

The same experts who can't fully explain human evolution will ridicule this theory and produce countless other experts to back them up. The author makes it clear this is a speculation, a hypothesis and unlike others, the author does not ask you to believe this or anything else you read in this book - only to do your own thinking. *Homo Antecessor* was a species of early humans that lived in Spain, France and Britain between 1.2 million and 800,000 years ago. Many scientists claim *Homo Antecessor* is the 'missing link' - the common ancestor of both modern man (*Homo Sapiens*) and Neanderthals. The author suggests that some of these early humans, who predated modern *Homo Sapiens* by hundreds of thousands of years, made it to the Emerald Isle where they evolved after a long period of genetic isolation. Red hair, blue eyes and milky-white skin are all thought to have evolved somewhere in the northern hemisphere as an adaptation to less intense sunlight. There is presently no physical evidence to support this 'Irish Evolution' theory however it must be remembered that Ireland is probably the most unexcavated place on earth. Hundreds of thousands of sites remain unexplored, with new ones being discovered every week. Countless bones and treasures lie beneath the mounds of Ireland. The author has included this theory as a clue for the free thinker who has long broken free from the chains of dogma. The evolution of Cro-Magnon man leads all the way back to the *Garden of Eden.*

Atlantis Ireland as a theory is based on the assumption that today's geologists are competent and know what they are doing. Geologists have mapped the entire Atlantic seabed and have been adamant for decades that a large sunken island does not exist anywhere in the Atlantic. These same geologists were able to map Zealandia and calculate that it was once a large continental island that sunk beneath the waves of the Pacific Ocean 23 million years ago. The suggestion they couldn't find a large island that apparently sank around 11,600 years ago lacks credibility. A tsunami is a much more logical explanation. New Zealand is all that remains of Zealandia today.

Deep sea divers were able to find the wreck of the *Titanic,* a feat considered impossible by many because it was like looking for a needle in a haystack. Yet despite numerous deep-sea expeditions a large sunken island in the Atlantic has not been found because it simply isn't there. Scientists know exactly how tectonic plates work and are adamant there is no large sunken island in the Atlantic. This is the primary reason why the legend of Atlantis has not been taken seriously by academics - they know a large sunken island in the Atlantic is not a viable theory. However, evidence has been stacking up to indicate a lost Atlantic mother culture and Ireland - an island in the Atlantic that does exist is a lot more viable explanation than an island that doesn't.

If a large sunken island in the Atlantic is ever discovered the author will be the first to concede that Ireland is merely a remnant of the Atlantian mother culture rather than the source. However, he has made the entirely reasonable assumption that the world's best geologists are competent and as a result he suggests that Ireland is the source of the *megalithic mother culture* that first sowed the first seeds of civilisation around the world.

The Romans who pillaged Egypt and Greece held very little sacred yet they described Ireland as *Insula Sacra - the sacred island.*

To the Romans, nothing was described as sacred unless it was extremely ancient. Ireland was known all around Europe as the *land of saints and scholars* long before the rise of the Vatican.

This Isle is sacred named by all the ancients, From times remotest in the womb of Chronos. This Isle which rises over the waves of ocean, is covered with a sod of rich luxuriance. And peopled far and wide by the Hiberni -Avienus, Roman Scholar

Power-hungry men have claimed to be gods, to speak for God, or to have a divine right to rule for thousands of years. Roman emperor Julius Caesar was murdered in 44 BC after being betrayed and stabbed in the back by several senators including his friend and protégé Brutus who became known as 'Brutus the Betrayer'. At Julius Caesar's funeral ceremony, the Romans declared that he was actually a god. In the month of July of the same year an extremely unusual comet known as Caesar's comet, was seen in the sky for seven days. The Romans believed that the comet was Caesar's soul ascending into heaven and the comet became a powerful propaganda tool that launched the career of Caesar's great-nephew (and adopted son) Augustus (also known as Octavian) who wished to become the Roman emperor.

However, Augustus had a big problem. Julius Caesar had one living son called Caesarion. Egyptian Pharaoh Cleopatra was his mother. In addition to becoming the Pharaoh of Egypt, Caesarion was also expected to succeed his father as the Roman Emperor and unite both empires, something that deeply troubled many Romans.

Both Caesarion and Cleopatra were declared as 'living gods' to the Egyptians. Caesarion was proclaimed to be the 'king of kings' and the 'son of God' while Cleopatra's influential Roman lover Marc Antony declared that Caesarion was Julius Caesar's true son and rightful heir to the Roman Empire. This declaration was a direct threat to Augustus (Octavian) whose claim to power was based on his status as Julius Caesar's grandnephew and adopted son. Shortly afterwards, Cleopatra and Marc Antony died in mysterious circumstances, while Caesarion was murdered by Roman soldiers acting on the orders of Augustus. After Caesarion's death, Egypt became part of the Roman Empire and was pillaged. Her temples were ransacked, her libraries destroyed and her civilisation fell.

Upon his death, Augustus was declared a god. His wife Livia was also declared a god upon her death. Declaring that people were gods was very fashionable at the time in Rome and claiming that you were a living god or that you spoke on behalf of God was a powerful tool to control the ignorant masses.

Rome was a pagan city for hundreds of years before 313 AD, when the Emperor Constantine issued the Edict of Milan, which recognised Christianity as one of many religions in Rome. Constantine proceeded to have his wife and his son murdered and deliberately postponed being baptised until on his deathbed in 337 AD, so that he could continue sinning and was still assured a heavenly afterlife by the priests. In 380 AD Christianity became the official religion of the Roman Empire who wanted a 'One Empire, One Emperor, One Religion' system of control.

The self-proclaimed Holy Roman Empire tried hard to destroy all the old religions and customs that threatened their claim to be divine rulers appointed by God. Everywhere they marched, they destroyed all evidence of previous civilisations and forced people to convert or die. Old pagan sites were demolished or repurposed as Christian sites. The Vatican itself is built on an old pagan site. Great pagan teachings, such as the works of Plato and Aristotle were labelled as blasphemy. In 392 AD the Roman Empire officially banned all pagan worship and events. Even the Olympic Games were banned.

A pagan was simply someone who did not believe official church dogma.

The destruction of the Great Library of Alexandria was one of the greatest crimes ever committed against humanity. The library was attacked and damaged several times before its final destruction by the Romans. Close to one million precious scrolls were destroyed, setting humanity back thousands of years.

Hypatia of Alexandria was a leading scientist, astronomer and philosopher at a time when women were considered second class citizens and the property of men. She was also considered the finest mathematician in the world. Hypatia was skinned alive and murdered by a Christian mob led by a lector named Peter. So savage was this mob that they carved the flesh from her bones and removed her eyes while she was still alive. The mob were followers of Cyril, the Bishop of Alexandria who according to renowned astronomer Carl Sagan, despised Hypatia because she was a woman who symbolised learning and science which were identified as paganism by the Roman church. Hypatia was all but forgotten by history. Rome declared Cyril a saint. Many scholars view Hypatia's murder as the birth of a dark age of ignorance where people were not allowed to think for themselves.

The story of the Roman Church is not a pleasant one to dwell upon. She made her advances by deception, forgery, war, persecution, torture, murder, ignorance and intolerance. The puppet kings of Europe were kept in power by the Vatican in an unholy alliance of greed, corruption and genocide that has spanned 1,700 years.

Millions were slaughtered across Europe. Millions more all around the world. The horrific scandals of recent times (child sex abuse, nuns forced into sex slavery, mass graves of children etc) are just the latest chapter in the history of the Vatican. In 2019, a group representing Irish sex abuse victims reported the Vatican to the International Criminal Court for crimes against humanity.

Thousands of scholars, scientists and free thinkers have been persecuted, burned at the stake, tortured, labeled as witches, anti-christs, heretics or pseudoscientists for daring to think for themselves. Since the beginning of time empires have preached love and peace while practicing hatred and genocide. Actions speak louder than words.

In 1155 AD Pope Adrian IV, an Englishman and head of the Roman Catholic church, authorised the English invasion of Ireland. The papal bull called *Laudabiliter* urged English King Henry II to invade Ireland to bring the *Independent Irish church* and the people of the island under the control of the Vatican.

Laudabiliter also granted the sovereignty of Ireland to King Henry II and requested that every Irish household pay the 'Peter's Pence' tax to Rome.

Up until the Vatican authorised the British invasion of Ireland, the Irish had an independent church.

Ireland took no part in the Vatican wars of the Crusades. The very absence of the Irish from the Crusades proves they did not belong to the Roman Church at that time. The Vatican had no authority in Ireland and sent the British to get it.

Eighteen successive kings of England, from Henry II (1171) until Henry VIII (1541), used the title 'Lord of Ireland' and claimed that it had been granted by Pope Adrian IV's successor, Pope Alexander III. For centuries attempts at sourcing the original *Laudabiliter* document have proved futile and the Vatican says the original papal bull is no longer in existence.

No papal degree was ever issued to contradict Laudabiliter.

Claims made across Europe that the Irish had lost their way was a deception to cover a land grab involving Roman popes, English kings and bleeding Irish hearts.

Ireland's ancient libraries, monasteries and culture have been desecrated over the centuries. Millions of books were burned by successive English invaders who, by destruction and forgery, have attempted to make it appear that Irish learning only started in the fourth century. Within a few centuries all traces of Irish education had been destroyed, her people left desolate and her ancient language driven to the very point of extinction.

As a species we are slowly climbing out of the slime of ignorance. For a long time, science was regarded as the enemy, freethinkers were traitors, and the intellectual progress of man was stunted. Every attempt was made to tarnish Ireland's ancient reputation and the reputation of great scholars throughout history like Hypatia, Bruno, Galileo, da Vinci, Plato and Aristotle - all of them 'pagans'.

There is no evidence whatsoever to support the myth that before the Roman invasion the British were savages. Who could equal the Romans themselves for savagery, as witnessed in the butcheries of the Colosseum, where every week people were fed alive to wild animals in front of thousands. These are the cultured Romans of the Classical Age which our academics so admire.

The world's ancient history has largely been written by bloodthirsty empires. It will come as no surprise to the impartial observer that Ireland's history has been written by her two great enemies - the mythmongers of Britain and Rome.

Because we focused on the snake, we missed the scorpion - African Proverb

Ogham Tree Alphabet

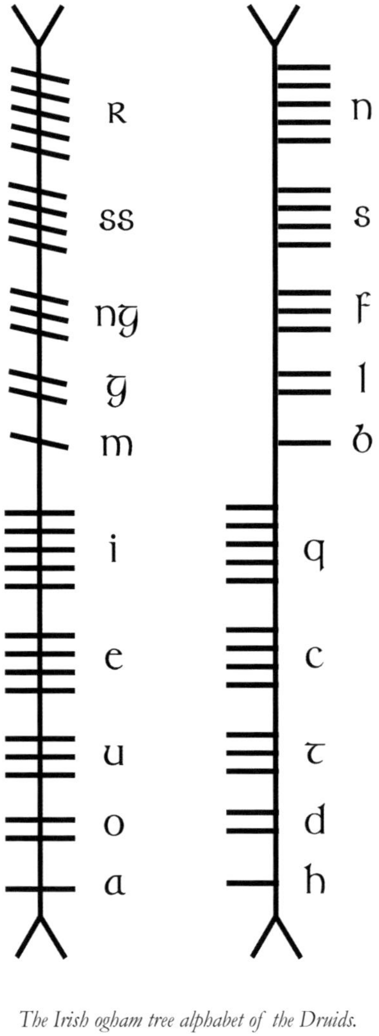

The Irish ogham tree alphabet of the Druids.
The original alphabet had 15 letters, each named after trees.

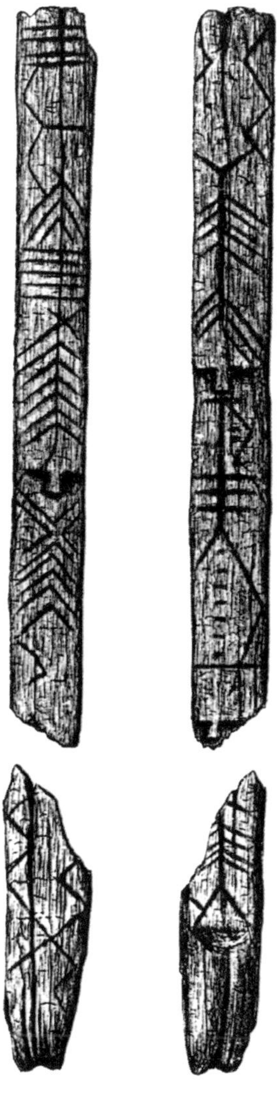

11,500-year-old Shigir Idol with ogham writing found in Siberia, Russia - Image Vladimir Tolmachev

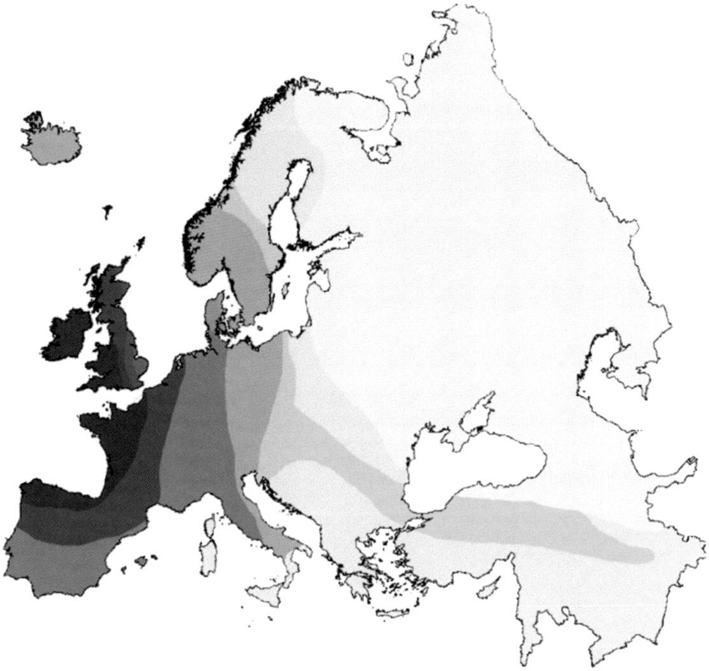

The highest concentration of Haplogroup R1b (direct descendent's of Cro-Magnon man) is found in Ireland

BRITAIN

We have always found the Irish to be a bit odd. They refuse to be English. - Winston Churchill

After the Vatican granted English King Henry II permission to invade Ireland, the British undertook the wholesale destruction of the Irish culture. Their ultimate aim was a 'final solution' to exterminate the Irish Gaelic race, and into Ireland they poured all their cruelty, all their corruption and all their hatred.

The looting of the island, destruction of her reputation and burning of her books left a smokescreen around Ireland's history which was forever meant to hide her great past and her priceless contribution to humanity. The British Empire, like the Roman father that spawned it, was built on deceit, forgery and slaughter while the generally accepted version of early Irish history is mostly fiction. Ireland's enemies wrote her history one lie at a time as her rivers ran red with blood. This inconvenient truth is not taught in many schools or universities.

In the following centuries the British unleashed unimaginable suffering on the Irish and drove her native language to the point of extinction. Having developed a taste for blood the British proceeded to rape, murder, and pillage their way across the entire world for centuries. Study the history of America, India, Australia, Africa, the Caribbean or anywhere else the British Empire plundered and you will observe the same 'scorched earth' policy summarised as follows - slaughter the natives, seize their land and rewrite their history.

George Orwell once likened Britain to a wealthy family with a guilty secret about the source of its wealth. How right he was. Here is the dark family secret, the skeleton in the empire's closet:

The British Empire sold millions into slavery and grew rich on the suffering of slaves

The history of British slavery has largely been brushed under the carpet while the thousands of British families who grew rich on the slave trade kept the source of their fortunes secret. After the abolition of slavery, the long distances between Britain, Africa and America made it possible for slavery to be largely airbrushed out of British history. The British transported millions of African slaves who were forcefully taken from their screaming families. As vast amounts of slaves poured into America, vast amounts of money poured into Britain. The British families who made fortunes from the slave trade built fine mansions, turned the city of London into the world's financial capital and established the Bank of England.

Slavery was not just the act of a few rogue traders, it was the official policy of the British government and went right to the throne. In 1663, King Charles II issued a *Royal Charter* granting a monopoly on the African slave trade to the *Royal African Company* which was owned by none other than himself and his cronies. With the help of the British military the *Royal African Company* established slave trading stations all along the African west coast.

The masterminds of the transatlantic slave trade sat on the British Throne

The *Royal African Company* was the world's biggest slave trader and was owned by none other than the British King Charles II and his cronies. Upon his death, control transferred to his Brother, James II who also became the King of England. The next king to sit on the throne was King Willian III (William of Orange) who also owned shares in the *Royal African Company* and benefited greatly from the proceeds of slavery.

Britain's royalty ran the world's biggest slave trading company and built fine palaces with the proceeds

The *Royal African Company* had a complete monopoly on the slave trade which they exploited to the full. Under the reign of King Willian III (William of Orange) the Westminster parliament passed the Africa Act, 1697 which opened up the slave trade to all English merchants. The volume of slave trading increased dramatically, and money poured into Britain as slave traders were encouraged by generous government subsidies that were approved by the so-called *right honourable gentlemen* in the Westminster parliament. This period marked the 'golden age' of the British Empire as fortunes were made, lords were appointed and fine palaces were built.

By the time Westminster finally passed the Slavery Abolition Act in 1833, there were *46,000 slave owners in Britain*, according to the Slave Compensation Commission, the government agency set up to *compensate the slave owners.*

The British government compensated 46,000 British slave owners for the loss of their property - 800,000 African slaves

The Slavery Abolition Act of 1833 formally freed 800,000 Africans who were then the legal property of Britain's 46,000 slave owners. This act provided *financial compensation to the slaveowners* for the loss of their 'property' and the compensation was paid for in full by the British taxpayer. £20 million was set aside to pay compensation, the modern equivalent of around £20 billion making it the biggest bailout in history until the 2009 banking crisis.

To add insult to injury, not only did the slaves not receive a single penny in compensation or an official apology, they had to *work four more years for free before their final liberation.*

In other words, while Britain's 46,000 slaveowners were handsomely compensated by the British taxpayer, the 800,000 slaves themselves had to work for free for another four long years before there were finally liberated. This arrangement was the work of the *right honourable gentlemen* in Westminster. Honourable indeed.

No official apology has ever been provided by Britain for the slave trade or several other crimes against humanity, probably due to the enormous financial compensation and embarrassment that would be involved.

The British who engaged in the conquest of Ireland were men as savage, ignorant and brutal as the world has ever seen. Wave after wave of tyrants crossed the Irish sea to plunder the sacred island. When an army of cut-throats meets a peaceful rural people there are few places to hide and the wailing cries of Ireland's children reached the very heavens. Ireland's wild geese were scattered to the four corners of the earth.

In 1531, Pope Clement VII sent a letter to King Henry VIII of England forbidding him to remarry. Henry ignored the Pope's warning and went on to marry the heavily pregnant Anne Boleyn (and four subsequent wives) leading to his excommunication. Henry VIII, the one-time defender of the Roman Catholic church across the British Empire now declared that the 'Vatican no longer had any authority' in England and took control of the Vatican's vast property empire in Britain. Henry used part of this enormous windfall to reward his cronies.

The Vatican had created a monster and lost all control of its spawn. The 'pro-Catholic' British crown had suddenly become 'anti-Catholic' having spent hundreds of years bringing Ireland's once *independent church* under the control of the Vatican. The 'Peter's Pence' taxes that the Irish were now paying to Rome were diverted to Britain. Since Ireland was now a Roman Catholic country within the now anti-Catholic British Empire it was caught in no-man's land. Having already endured several centuries of persecution, worse was to follow.

The British introduced the *Penal Laws* which officially made Irish Catholics *second class citizens* in their own land. These laws, which lasted for centuries, can only be described as ethnic cleansing that further reduced a once wise nation, a land of saints and scholars, to a state of ignorance, poverty and despair. These laws, along with the deliberate tarnishing of Ireland's reputation, fuelled the fires of British racism that were directed against the Irish, a fire that still smoulders.

It (the Penal Laws) is a machine …as well fitted for the oppression, impoverishment and degradation of a people, and the debasement in them of human nature itself, as ever proceeded from the perverted ingenuity of man - Edmund Burke, MP

Gentlemen, you may soon have the alternative to live as slaves or die as free men. - Daniel O'Connell

This is a righteous judgement of God upon these barbarous wretches - Oliver Cromwell

Here is an outline of the Penal Laws which were approved by the *right honourable gentlemen* of Westminster:

- *The Irish Catholic was forbidden the exercise of his religion.*
- *He was forbidden to receive education.*
- *He was forbidden to enter a profession.*
- *He was forbidden to hold public office.*
- *He was forbidden to engage in trade or commerce.*
- *He was forbidden to live in a corporate town or within five miles thereof.*
- *He was forbidden to own a horse of greater value than five pounds.*
- *He was forbidden to own land.*
- *He was forbidden to lease land.*
- *He was forbidden to accept a mortgage on land in security for a loan.*
- *He was forbidden to vote.*
- *He was forbidden to keep any arms for his protection.*
- *He was forbidden to hold a life annuity.*
- *He was forbidden to buy land from a Protestant.*
- *He was forbidden to receive a gift of land from a Protestant.*
- *He was forbidden to inherit land from a Protestant.*
- *He was forbidden to inherit anything from a Protestant.*
- *He was forbidden to rent any land that was worth more than 30 shillings a year.*
- *He was forbidden to reap from his land any profit exceeding a third of the rent.*
- *He could not be guardian to a child.*
- *He could not, when dying, leave his infant children under Catholic guardianship.*
- *He could not attend Catholic worship.*
- *He was compelled by law to attend Protestant worship.*
- *He could not himself educate his child.*
- *He could not send his child to a Catholic teacher.*
- *He could not employ a Catholic teacher to come to his child.*
- *He could not send his child abroad to receive education.*

These laws were clearly designed to exterminate the Irish race, a long-held ambition of the British establishment and in 1845 they got a chance for their *final solution.*

As a result of the Penal Laws and 700 years of genocide the native Irish had been reduced to living in complete poverty. Having been kicked off their own land, potatoes became a staple of the diet as they could be grown on the side of the road and on tiny parcels of land. When the European potato blight disease reached Ireland much of the native food supply stopped. Although the potato crop failed other crops such as wheat and barley thrived. During this period Ireland produced millions of tons of food which was shipped to Britain by the boatload.

The primary cause of the huge death toll was not potato blight - it was food removal. Millions of tons of food was exported from Ireland during An Gorta Mór - the Great Hunger.

Internationally, the famine was portrayed by the British as an unfortunate natural event to conceal the truth - the primary cause of the massive death toll was the removal of food from Ireland by the British army. The famine was a starvation, a holocaust, a deliberate policy of brutality to exterminate the Irish - Britain's *final solution.*

At least one million died and another million emigrated. The native Irish starved as they watched boatloads of food leave their country in what can only be described as the greatest act of genocide in the 19th century.

According to British military records over half of the entire British army were stationed in Ireland during the famine period. Their role was to transport food and protect it from the starving natives, assist with evictions and other horrific activities reminiscent of the Nazis. Ireland is covered in mass graves from this period.

The famine was a deliberate policy of starvation to achieve Britain's long held goal of exterminating the Irish race - its final solution.

Famine was a low-cost military strategy that the British used all around the world because it was easy to hide and cheaper than bullets. Edmund Spencer, the great English poet and British government official campaigned vigorously for the extermination of the Irish race and suggested famine as the means. Arthur Chichester, England's Viceroy to Ireland also campaigned for famine as the military means to exterminate the Irish race.

I have often said, and written, it is famine which must consume them - Arthur Chichester, England's Viceroy to Ireland

The legacy of slavery and racism still poisons large parts of the planet today. In addition to African slaves, the British transported million of 'indentured servants' - a more politically acceptable term for slave labour. Millions of Indians were transported from India to the Caribbean as indentured labour. Hundreds of thousands of Irish were sent to the Caribbean and Australia against their will. Enslaved Africans that were taken to Britain were often sold as 'indentured servants' and were advertised in the *London Post* and other newspapers as 'Slaves for sale'.

Indentured servants could be bought and sold, forced into labour, and were subject to extreme physical punishment and cruelty. While there were some technical differences between 'indentured servants' and 'slaves' the net effect was the same.

An indentured servant had virtually no rights, an African slave had none.

Indentured labour, also known as 'debt bondage' was a system to provide free slave labour to the British Empire.

There can be absolutely no argument that 'indentured servants' were slaves. In 1948, the United Nations issued a Universal Declaration of Human Rights which recognised and banned 'indentured labour' as a form of slavery.

After the trans-Atlantic slave trade had ended *slavery still remained legal* in the British Empire once the slave was a convicted criminal. Tens of thousands of Irishmen were enslaved and shipped to Australia as convicts, having been found guilty under the Penal Laws of such petty crimes as speaking their native language or stealing food to feed their starving families. As well as removing millions of tons of food from Ireland during the famine, the British Army also removed thousands of convicts until the last prison ship sailed to Australia in 1868, 18 years after the famine holocaust. The world-famous Irish song *The Fields of Athenry* was written about Irish enslavement during the famine. Ireland's valleys fell silent, except for the cries of the last starving child. There was no laughter.

Hundreds of thousands of Irish men, women and children were sent to the Caribbean, particularly Barbados and Montserrat, as slave labour. Many women and children were forced into sex slavery. The British settlers found that the Irish slaves were not as well suited to labour in the tropics as the African slaves, who were less affected by tropical diseases like malaria. As a result, a male African slave was worth approximately £50 pounds sterling while female Irish slaves were so plentiful they were often free for the taking. The British planters soon began a slave breeding program. They would breed an African male slave with as many Irish female slaves as they could get their hands on, as the mixed-race offspring could still be sold for top dollar. A premium was paid for pretty mixed-race slave girls whose light brown skin was considered more attractive and rarer than the plentiful black African or white Irish sex slaves. Children suffered just as much as adults. Paedophilia was rampant. In 1656, Oliver Cromwell ordered 2,000 Irish children to be taken to Jamaica and *sold as slaves* to British planters.

A statue honouring Oliver Cromwell still stands outside the Westminster parliament where he was once a member, a fine palace on the banks of the Thames that was built with the proceeds of slavery.

The past has a habit of bursting unto the stage when it's least expected and lying about its history is a British pastime. The British Foreign Office has been *unlawfully concealing* 1.2 million historical files at a highly secure government compound at Hanslope Park - a maximum-security outpost 50 miles north of London. These files contain millions of records stretching back to 1662, covering the entire slave trade, the American war of Independence, the Battle of the Boyne, the Irish famine, the Boer wars, two World Wars, the Cold War and numerous other events. It also includes thousands of records of British colonial activities in Ireland from the time of Cromwell up to and including the troubles.

In a separate military warehouse at Swadlincote in southern Derbyshire, more than 66,000 Ministry of Defence files are being stored *despite the British Governments legal obligation to release them* under the Freedom of Information Act. These military archives include documents from the 1970s and early 80s, some of the most bloody and controversial years of the Irish Troubles.

Despite pledges in 2011 from the right honourable gentlemen in Westminster that these files would be released, almost 10 years later the files are still withheld - despite the British governments legal obligation to release them.

The British government recently paid compensation to 5,200 Kenyans who had been tortured during the Mau Mau uprising in the 1950s. The Kenya Human Rights Commission has estimated 90,000 Kenyans were killed or maimed and 160,000 imprisoned during the uprising. The prisoners, which included women and children, suffered appalling treatment including rape, castration, torture and murder while detained in British *concentration camps.* In

1957, Britain's own attorney general in Kenya described these *concentration camps* as being reminiscent of the Nazis.

One of the prisoners was Hussein Onyango Obama, grandfather of US President Barack Obama.

After Kenya achieved independence in 1963, the British destroyed mountains of documents in an attempt to hide all evidence of their many crimes against humanity. Similar evidence destruction, codenamed Project Legacy, occurred in numerous British colonies around the world. The objective of Project Legacy was 'to destroy any files that could embarrass her majesty's government'. For decades the British claimed that absolutely no legacy documents remained however in 2011 the British Government finally admitted that it held millions of top secret 'watch files' in Hanslope Park which they had apparently 'forgotten about'. A handful of these explosive files were eventually released to Kenyan lawyers in 2012 for an ongoing Mau Mau legal case. London tried for three years to block the Mau Mau veterans' legal action in the courts. Britain first argued that responsibility for events during the uprising passed to Kenya upon its independence in 1963, an argument which the courts rejected. The British government then said the claim was brought long after the legal time limit. However, a judge ruled that as there was *ample documentary evidence* a fair trial was possible.

In 2012 a London court ruled that the victims could sue Britain for its crimes against humanity, a case which they won. This ruling has set a legal precedent.

It is the opinion of the author that the British Empire is guilty of numerous crimes against humanity and that it owes reparations, financial compensation to the descendants of colonialism and the slave trade all around the world. Mountains of evidence to support such claims are stored in British military warehouses at Hanslope Park and Swadlincote. Should these millions of descendants ever seek reparations in a group legal action the total compensation would be trillions of pounds and could very well break the Bank of England - a bank founded with the proceeds of the slave trade.

The Battle of the Boyne played a big part in the Catholic versus Protestant division that still poisons Ireland today. This battle was not fought between Catholics and Protestants nor between the English and the Irish. It was fought as the result of a *military partnership* between the Vatican and William of Orange.

War is an expensive business and cash-strapped William's military campaign, his so called 'glorious revolution' was almost certainly financed by Pope Innocent XI via his rich Odescalchi banking family. When news of William's victory in Ireland reached Rome, the Vatican was lit up in celebration.

The Vatican celebrated the victory of William of Orange in Ireland and held a special thanksgiving mass in his honour.

Few of Ireland's Orangemen realise that William of Orange was a Vatican puppet and it pleased the Vatican tremendously to have him sit on the British throne as King William III of England. William was also a slave trader and slave owner who benefited enormously from the slave trade. He even had a statue made of his favourite male slave and suspected lover which is displayed in the Royal Kensington Palace today. This statue is still kept inside a cage.

King Billy, as he is known in Ireland, was a slave trader and military ally of the Vatican. He was also rumoured to have had several male lovers.

The Irish national flag, the Tricolour, is green, white and orange to represent peace between both main traditions on the island - the Nationalist mostly Catholic 'green' and the Unionist mostly Protestant 'orange'. Nationalists viewed the Vatican as its friend and British Empire as its enemy, while Unionists viewed the British Empire as its friend and Vatican as its enemy. Both were deceived.

The brutal truth is Ireland has had two great enemies not one - Rome and Britain. Like father, like son.

The Orange Unionist tradition in Ireland has always despised the Vatican because they knew things about Rome the Nationalists didn't. The original meaning of the famous phrase *No Surrender* was actually *No Surrender to Rome.*

Because we were focused on the snake we missed the scorpion - African Proverb

Geoffrey of Monmouth was one of the greatest scholars ever produced by Wales. In his crowning work - *The History of the Kings of Britain* - he describes how the rocks of Stonehenge were healing rocks called the 'Giants' Ring' or the 'Giants Dance', which giants had originally brought *from Africa to Ireland* for their healing properties and that Merlin the wizard along with King Uther Pendragon (King Arthurs Father) and 15,000 soldiers took the stones from Ireland after slaughtering 7,000 Irish.

Another British legend involving the heel stone at Stonehenge described how the giant stones were taken from Ireland and how the true origin of the stones would never be found out. We will probably never know for sure where the giant stones really came from however what makes these legends so interesting is they are from credible *British sources.*

Henges are found all across Ireland and Britain. *Dronehenge* is a nickname given to a huge Irish monument discovered in 2018. Its 154m diameter makes it the *largest known henge on earth.* It has yet to be excavated.

'Send for the Giants Ring (Stonehenge) which is on Mount Killaraus in Ireland' said Merlin - Geoffrey of Monmouth

According to Geoffrey of Monmouth, Britain was founded by the Greek Brutus of Troy after he defeated the giants who were the only inhabitants of Britain, which at the time was called Albion. Brutus then established his capital *Troia Nova* (New Troy) on the banks of the Thames which was later renamed London. Brutus also named the island 'Britain' after himself.

Brutus of Troy was well known in medieval England as the first king of Britain. Brutus of Troy is not the same Brutus who stabbed Julies Caesar in the back - that was 'Brutus the Betrayer', best known for the phrase 'even you, Brutus', the last words spoken by Julius Caesar after his best friend Brutus had *stabbed him in the back.*

The modern words 'brute' and 'brutality' are derived from the name Brutus. The dictionary definition of a brute is *a savagely violent person or someone displaying an absence of intelligence.*

Let us hope Geoffrey was wrong when he told the world that Britain was named after Brutus, or it will forever be associated with betrayal and brutality. Either way, there is no hiding the brutality of the British Empire in Africa, America, India, Ireland or anywhere else they plundered.

We conquered India by the sword and by the sword we shall hold it. I am not such a hypocrite to say we hold India for the Indians
- British Home Secretary 1928

The story of the British Empire in India is another horrific tale of oppression. The county was simply bled dry by the empire for centuries. Up to 35 million died unnecessarily in famines as boatloads of food were removed from India by the *men without souls* in yet another famine holocaust that was cheaper than bullets. It was their own fault, according to Churchill who famously 'hated Indians' whom he described as 'a beastly people'. However, he didn't hate the Indians enough not to borrow £1.25 billion from them during World War II. This debt *still hasn't been paid back* by the right honourable gentlemen in Westminster. Honourable indeed.

It is not because I hate the British, I hate only the Empire - Gandhi

The further you run from your crimes the more exhausted you are when they finally catch up with you. And catch up with you they do. Such was the brutality of the British colonists they became known all around the world as the *men without souls.*

The British Empire was far from the great and glorious bringer of civilisation it claims to have been, it was a destroyer of civilisations, an empire of cut-throats, slave traders and tyrants.

An empire so bloodthirsty its flag was called the butchers apron.

An empire so brutal it became rich on the suffering of slaves.

An empire so bankrupt it wrote history one lie at a time.

An empire so arrogant it still calls itself great.

The British Empire poured all its cruelty, all its corruption and all its hatred into Ireland, yet despite everything the Irish don't hate them. The only revenge they seek is the laughter of their children.

The sun never sets on the British Empire because even God couldn't trust an Englishman in the dark
- Shashi Tharoor

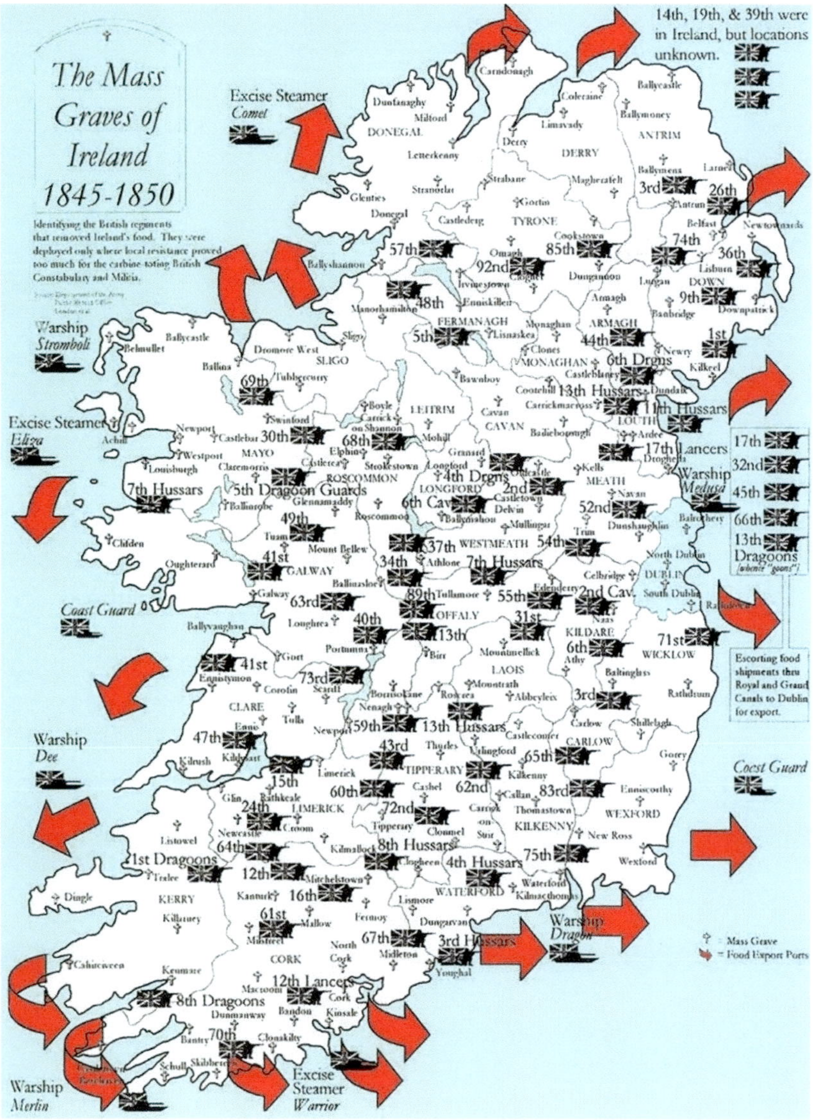

The mass graves of Ireland - Image Chris Fogarty, The Perfect Holocaust

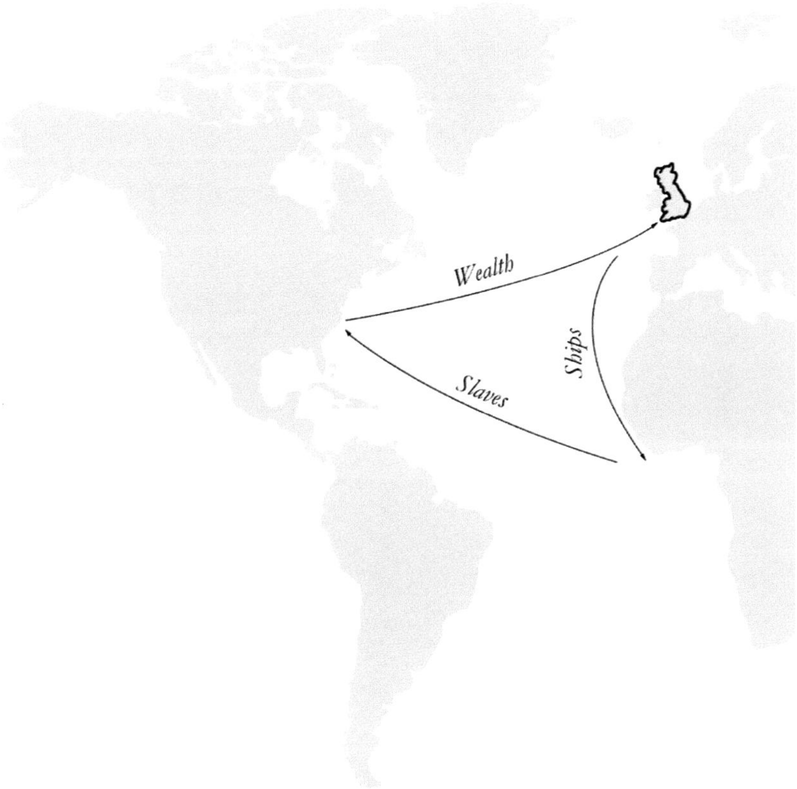

Britain's slavery triangle

'Bust of an enslaved man' - the statue of William of Orange / King William III's favourite male slave is still kept in a cage in Kensington Palace - Image RCT

IRELAND

They say the clouds are lower in Ireland. I say Ireland is closer to Heaven.
- Michael Vatis

Ireland is probably the most unexcavated place on earth. There is barely a townland in the entire island that doesn't have a Stone Age construction of some description. Every corner of the Emerald Isle is littered with relics of the ancient past that have yet to be investigated. It truly is a time capsule waiting to be opened.

The Hill of Tara was the seat of the High King of Ireland and has around 100 unexcavated structures including the remains of a giant 6,000-sq-m banqueting hall.

Imagine what treasures lie beneath the famous hill.

Brú na Bóinne, the site of Newgrange has around 200 unexcavated structures including the biggest henge on earth which is twice the width of Stonehenge.

Imagine how spectacular it will look when its restored to its former glory.

The entire island of Ireland has around 100,000 Stone Age structures that have never been excavated.

Imagine all the historical artefacts that have yet to be discovered.

The most spectacular Stone Age constructions on the entire planet are found on the Emerald Isle. This alone is enough to prove that long before the pyramids were constructed, the ancient Irish had an advanced civilisation that was thousands of years ahead of its time.

The Newgrange mound contains an estimated 200,000 tons of material that was moved to and around the site. Its estimated that construction would have taken 30 years using a workforce of around 300 highly skilled master builders, stonemasons and architects. Newgrange was built using astonishing boats that transported 5 - 10 ton boulders to the site. Imagine the level of intelligence needed to load and unload such giant rocks, let alone the skill needed to engineer a boat capable of carrying such enormous weights. The boulders were of a particular type of rock called *greywacke* which is only found in one place in Ireland - the shoreline at Clogherhead, County Louth. The only route to transport the stones to Newgrange was to sail several kilometres in the open sea as far as the mouth of the river Boyne and from there sail the remainder of the journey against the current of the river. This entire 30km journey was repeated close to 100 times and required the ability to sail in the open sea and against the current of the river - a remarkable achievement. A Stone Age quay and boats have recently been found at the site several meters below ground level.

Newgrange is the most famous of Ireland's ancient monuments and is steeped in legend. It was built by the magical *Tuatha Dé Danann.* It is the *circular* Temple of Atlantis that Plato described as being half a stadia wide and having a strange barbaric appearance. Half a stadia is 83m while Newgrange is 85m wide, an almost perfect match. Newgrange is also the sacred Temple of the Hyperboreans from Greek mythology which was described as being a magnificent *circular* temple that was located on a fertile island with swans, priests with harps and an unusually temperate climate. The Greeks described how Hyperborea was governed by the Boreadae. *Boreadach* is an Irish word which means noble chieftain or wise leader. Ireland clearly is the Greek island of Hyperborea.

Newgrange is the most famous of many sites located at Brú na Bóinne on the banks of the river Boyne in County Meath. The nearby mound at Knowth is equally impressive. Brú na Bóinne contains at least 200 unexcavated structures. More are being found every year.

Newgrange is older than Stonehenge, older than the pyramids and the author is absolutely certain that Newgrange and the Brú na Bóinne site will be proven to be much older than the 11,000 year old Gobekli Tepe when some of the 200 or so structures at the site are actually excavated. A 400,0000-year-old stone tool was found nearby in Mell, Drogheda, County Louth and more will surely follow.

Time will prove that Newgrange and the entire Brú na Bóinne site is substantially older than current estimates.

Ireland's Stone Age constructions were built to align with the heavens, particularly the sun, which the ancients considered to be the shining face of God. They watched its every move and divided the year into the light and dark half. The winter solstice (shortest day of the year) was a time for huge celebration because it signalled the start of a new year when days would get longer, and food would be more plentiful. Every December at the winter solstice the sun reaches its lowest point in the sky which the ancients interpreted as the *death of the sun* who had grown weaker and weaker and was finally defeated by the darkness, whom it had battled all year.

At the winter solstice on December 21st, the sun stands still in the sky for three days before it rises again on December 25th. The glorious resurrection of the sun was a cause for huge celebration. The ancient Irish celebrated Christmas (*Nollaig*) as the *rebirth of the unconquerable sun* and exchanged gifts long before the pagan celebration was hijacked and turned into a Christian feast. The Newgrange mound represented the womb and the light entering the passage at the winter solstice represented the seed fertilising the womb. Mother Earth was symbolically fertilised by Father Heaven and nine months later the crops were harvested. The ancients honoured the sun because they knew it was vital for all life on earth and they considered it to be the shining face of God. Irish ogham writing found in America described the sun as being the 'eye of God'. Hundreds of Irish Stone Age constructions are aligned to the solstices, equinoxes and other celestial movements proving the early Irish had obtained a truly stunning knowledge of mathematics, construction and astronomy.

The Irish Druids were master astronomers and were the first people to understand the movement of the heavens, such as the cycles of the sun, the moon and the stars. Understanding the cycles of the sun and the moon were particularly important for agriculture, while knowledge of the stars was extremely important for sailing and navigation.

The early Irish astronomers carved images of an ancient solar eclipse into giant stones at Loughcrew in County Meath over 5,300 years ago, on November 30, 3340 BC to be exact. This is the oldest known recorded solar eclipse in history, predating the next closest recording on earth by almost 2,000 years. This level of knowledge is truly astonishing.

The ancient Egyptians, Indians and Persians were all fully aware of the 25,920-year cycle called the *precession of the equinox*, which is also known as the Great Year. This knowledge could not have been developed over a few centuries or even a millennia or two - this incredibly precise knowledge could only have been developed over tens of thousands of years and this ancient knowledge came from the Druids of old Ireland.

Astronomy started in Ireland and it was the Druids who gave the Milky Way its name - they called it the *Way of the White Cow*. Cows and rivers played a huge part in Irish mythology and the white cow was highly treasured. Ireland's astronomers regarded the Milky Way as a heavenly reflection of the River Boyne - as above, so below.

It was in old Ireland that primitive man first rose out of a state of barbarism and built a civilisation that was ahead of its time. Language, agriculture, metalwork, mathematics, philosophy, astronomy, construction, music, poetry, and science were all first developed in ancient Ireland. Claims made by Ireland's enemies that education, mathematics and writing were first introduced in the fourth century was propaganda and a complete falsehood. Stone Age masterpieces like Newgrange couldn't possibly have been built by people who didn't have language, letters, numbers and a remarkable knowledge of astronomy.

One of the greatest myths relating to Ireland is that it fully froze over during the last Ice Age - it didn't.

Ireland was *never* completely frozen over - even at the very peak of the Ice Age only some of the island was under ice sheets. The implications of this are enormous. Ireland's Stone Age history has been written on the false assumption that the island was completely frozen over for the entire Ice Age which is complete nonsense. Because Ireland is heated all year round by the warm Atlantic Gulf Stream, the island has a very temperate climate that avoids the extremes. Both winters and summers are much milder than virtually anywhere else on earth.

Scientists have now proven that the Atlantic Gulf Stream did not stop during the Ice Age as was previously thought.

Since the Gulf Stream did not stop, Ireland's Ice Age was not as extreme as previous estimates. Ireland has over 1,000 species of native flora and fauna. It also has unique *freshwater fish* that are not found anywhere else on earth which can only be explained by the island not fully freezing over during the Ice Age.

Many of these unique species evolved in Ireland - an isolated ocean island - the perfect place for rapid evolution and quantum leaps.

The Ice Age lasted from around 2.6 million years ago until around 11,600 years ago and reached its peak around 22,000 years ago when temperatures started rising again, apart from a sudden *unexplained* mini Ice Age, called the Younger Dryas period, which lasted from around 12,800 to 11,600 years ago. When the Younger Dryas mini Ice Age ended so did the Great Ice Age.

This mini Ice Age started with a period of *rapid global cooling* and ended with a period of *rapid global warming.*

The sheer speed of the cooling and warming has completely baffled scientists for decades and is still considered a mystery. What has also bamboozled scientists is that both these periods of rapid cooling and warming were accompanied by massive flooding events which scientists call Meltwater Pulse 1A and 1B. So far, a scientific explanation has not been agreed upon.

The author suggests that that the Younger Dryas mini Ice Age was triggered by earth encountering a comet swarm, with a particularly large comet striking Greenland which melted huge amounts of ice causing a sudden drop in global temperatures and was ended when a second comet struck the Atlantic ocean at the Puerto Rico trench. *This second event boiled the ocean.*

Cosmic impacts unleash a huge amount of energy and are a lot more frequent in earth's history than science likes to admit. As recently as 1908, in Tunguska, Siberia a cosmic impact released 15 Megatons of energy - the equivalent of 1,000 Hiroshima atomic bombs. This event flattened an estimated 80 million trees like matchsticks over an area of 2,150 km^2. This was a relatively small cosmic event compared to others in the past although had it stuck a large city like Moscow or New York, the city would cease to exist.

Gravitational anomalies often indicate large impact craters and the Puerto Rico Trench has the most negative gravitational anomaly on earth.

According to NASA, beneath the Puerto Rico trench is a mass so dense its gravitational pull causes the ocean to dip and it affects navigational instruments. The Puerto Rico trench is also located in the infamous Bermuda Triangle.

The author suggests this is the remains of a huge comet, which the ancients called a 'fiery dragon' or an 'evil serpent', that unleashed hell on earth. The site contains the deepest point in the entire Atlantic Ocean. As this site is so close to tectonic plate boundaries, a comet impact here would trigger global earthquakes, volcanoes and tsunamis. As the oceans boiled, huge quantities of steam would have reached the atmosphere causing torrential rainfall lasting for months. Volcanos would have erupted all over the world while the tectonic plates would have shaken causing numerous earthquakes. A series of giant tsunamis would have affected most of the world including Atlantis Ireland. These events are the origin of the 'great flood' legends found in virtually every tradition on earth. We will all have to wait for the science to catch up to prove or disprove this theory.

The old Stone Age is the period before the end of the Ice Age, around 11,600 years ago. It is widely believed by academics that Ireland was not inhabited by humans during this time, however this is incorrect. A 12,500-year-old bear bone found in County Clare that was cut by a human tool proves there were humans in Ireland during the Old Stone Age.

The author suggests that *Ireland has been inhabited by humans for hundreds of thousands of years,* more than enough time to develop an advanced Stone Age civilisation, and the evidence is there to prove it if academics would just open their eyes. Despite Ireland being the most under-excavated place on earth, three separate finds of old Stone Age tools dating from 200,000 - 400,000 years ago have already been made and there is no logical reason to suspect humans weren't in Ireland from 400,000 years ago until now, if not from an even earlier date. The author also expects several new finds in the next decade, particularity in the Waterford Estuary and Boyne Valley regions to confirm this claim.

However, based on the false assumption that Ireland was completely frozen over during the Ice Age, academics have offered the bizarre explanation that these Old Stone Age tools were brought to Ireland by ice sheets. When similar tools were found in Britain, academics declared they were proof of human habitation. This ludicrous double standard is based on the false belief that Ireland was uninhabitable during the Ice Age and goes to show the main problem with academics - they are specialists - highly educated in one area with very little knowledge of any other fields. For example, most archaeologists don't know the first thing about astronomy, geology, mythology, psychology or any other 'ology' you can think of. As a result, they are unable to join the dots and are hopelessly shackled by mainstream opinion.

It's only by studying many different fields that patterns are found and you can then join the dots. Study the records of the world's greatest minds, the geniuses who have walked the earth and you will discover that while they had specialist knowledge they were not specialists, they were generalists, polymaths who studied anything they could get their hands on to help them join the dots.

You can't join the dots if you can't see them.

The greatest breakthroughs man has ever made were the earliest and agriculture was probably the most spectacular gift ever given to humanity. With a reliable food supply, people could build a civilisation. The cultivation of crops is something that would have taken early man many thousands of years to develop. Cereals are the edible grains of grass plants. Oats, wheat and barley crops were first developed in Ireland by selectively breeding wild grasses to maximise the yield. The original grasses, such as meadow barley, that were first cultivated in Ireland still exist there in the wild and genetic testing can prove this theory. Cereals were the building blocks of all the world's great civilisations - Persia, Egypt, Greece, Rome and Britain were all built on them. Without great cereals there was no great civilisations.

It is often claimed that cereal crops were first developed in the Fertile Crescent - the so-called 'cradle of civilisation' that runs from the Nile valley to the Middle East however this seems dubious. The Fertile Crescent is next door to the Sahara Desert and at the end of the last Ice Age 11,600 years ago, the Sahara Desert was just as dry as it is today. But sandwiched in-between the two periods of extreme dryness were a few thousand years of plentiful rainfall called the African Humid period. It seems much more likely that agriculture had already been developed somewhere else more suitable and then taken to the Fertile Crescent region at a later date.

An island is the perfect place for evolution and the development of a civilisation. Crops were first developed in Ireland tens of thousands of years ago and as agriculture on the island was impacted by the Ice Age, some people left seeking new lands taking the skill of agriculture and a supply of seeds with them. Ancient seeds found in the Fertile Crescent can be genetically compared with Irish seeds to prove or disprove this claim.

The oldest agricultural fields on earth are Ireland's Ceide Fields. Various trees grew at Ceide Fields which provided firewood, building materials and food. Ancient ploughs, farming tools and quern stones used for milling flour have all been found at the site, as have livestock pens.

These fields were found *below a peat bog* which means they were agricultural fields long before the bog developed on top of them, implying a very ancient origin. How old does something need to be for a bog to form on top of it and what sort of natural event would need to happen to form such a bog?

Ireland's temperate climate, lack of predators and isolation made it perfect for the development of agriculture which began on the Emerald Isle with the domestication of cattle, horses, deer, goats, sheep, pigs, fowl and wolfhounds.

The ancient Irish used charcoal to create highly fertile soil and bought this technique to the world. Charcoal traps nutrients and is a breeding ground for soil bacteria which is essential for soil health. In South America the soil that this technique creates is called *Terra Preta* which means dark earth and according to South American legends, this knowledge was taken to them by bearded red or fair-haired strangers. Charcoal, water and soil bacteria can turn even sand into fertile soil. Charcoal, often called biochar, can even be added to the diet of modern cattle to reduce methane emissions and aid digestion.

Quern-stones were developed to mill grains into flour. As the ancient Irish had access to fire, flour, milk, water and eggs, they were able to make bread all year round. Stores of vegetables, apples and hazelnuts were also vitally important winter rations. Herbs were also grown and used as foods, medicines and ointments.

The early Irish made butter, cream and cheese from the milk of cows and goats which they stored in cold bogs and underground pits.

4,000-year-old bog butter has recently been discovered in Ireland. It was still edible.

Food was often a community affair. A *fulacht fiadh* was a stone pit used to boil water to cook meats and stews for the tribe. Stones were heated in a blazing fire before being placed into the water to boil. Ingredients were then added to the water to make a giant stew for the community. *Fulacht Fiadhs* were also used for the washing and dying of cloth, the working of leather and for bathing. *Fulacht Fiadhs*, also known as 'burnt mounds' have been found in Britain, Sweden and Switzerland. Thousands are found across Ireland.

The ancient Irish were master fishermen and this provided year-round food as did hunting. The eel was a particularly important source of highly nutritious fats and vitamin C. The ancient Irish also farmed kelp - a vitamin-rich seaweed which can produce 4 tons of crop per acre of sea while Boyne river curraghs (coracles) have been used to fish for river salmon since the Stone Age.

It was in ancient Ireland that cattle were first domesticated. Cattle were used for milk, meat and to pull ploughs. Lactose tolerance is the ability to break down the sugar in non-human milk such as cow's milk. Ireland has the highest concentration of lactose tolerance on earth along with Denmark, only 5% of the Irish are lactose intolerant, a resistance that has been developed over many thousands of years indicating that the Irish drank cow's milk from the earliest of times. In ancient Ireland, cows were prized possessions. Wealth was not measured by gold, silver or even land but by head of cattle and the more cattle you had the wealthier you were. The milk (*milch*) cow was the highest unit of currency under Ireland's ancient Brehon laws.

It was also in Ancient Ireland that horses were first tamed and bred. The Irish Hobby horse provided the foundation bloodlines for the modern Thoroughbred racehorse and several other breeds. DNA origin studies show that 68% of the modern Thoroughbred is derived from the Irish Hobby - its closest genetic relative. Put simply, the fastest horses on the planet get their speed from the Irish Hobby horse.

Man sailed a boat long before he saddled a horse. After the ancients had mastered sailing on Ireland's lakes and rivers, they took to the high seas. During the construction of Newgrange, 5 - 10 ton-boulders were transported to the site by boat in the open sea and against the river current. A boat capable of carrying such an enormous weight is more than capable of sailing the high seas and Irish mythology has numerous stories of epic voyages to far flung lands.

The Irish Druids passed their ancient wisdom *from mouth to ear,* believing that to write sacred wisdom was to desecrate it and that each future translation and interpretation would further dilute it. Throughout history many brilliant minds have walked the earth sharing wisdom, yet ignorant men *have mutilated their simple message beyond all recognition.* Simplicity is the essence of genius, any idiot can make things complicated.

The development of the first language was a long and slow process that occurred over many thousands of years. The ancient Irish Gaelic language has almost one million words while most of the world's languages have less than two hundred thousand. This is all the more remarkable when you consider the ancient Irish language has been driven to the point of extinction and has not been in everyday use in most parts of Ireland for centuries. The Penal Laws were designed to exterminate Irish culture and the punishment for even speaking the native language was death.

Calvert Watkins was a professor of linguistics at Harvard University and one of the world's leading experts on the origin of languages. Watkins concluded that Old Irish Gaelic is an extraordinary ancient language and the closest to the first language - the famous 'missing mother tongue'. All the world's languages are descended from one mother tongue - Old Irish Gaelic. It is not a branch of the world language tree as most academics think, it is the very root and displays remarkable similarities to the oldest languages on the planet including Hebrew, Sanskrit, Arabic, Chaldean and Native American tongues.

There is also a great similarity between the alphabets of the ancient world showing a definite link. Ogham, the ancient Irish tree alphabet of the Druids is the oldest alphabet in the world and not only predates other codes of writing, it is as old as the Stone Age itself. Ogham was called a tree alphabet because each letter was named after a tree and several letters from the world's oldest alphabets are still named after trees. Ogham writing has been found in several locations across North America, on a stone in the Hanging Gardens of Babylon and on an ancient Arabic text found in Egypt. Just like the ogham tree alphabet, each of the Chaldean and Hebrew letters derived its name from a tree or shrub. In 'Anacalypsis' by Godfrey Higgins we learn that the letters of the Hebrew alphabet were named after Irish trees.

Ogham writing is also found on the Shigar idol, an 11,500-year-old wooden carving discovered in Siberia, Russia.

Ogham writing features heavily in Irish mythology where it's said to have been invented by Ogma, a member of the *Tuatha Dé Danann* - Ireland's magical 'Tribe of the Gods' who in one legend arrived in *ships from the sky*.

The two main tribes in Irish mythology are the *Fomorians* and the *Tuatha Dé Danann*. The Fomorains were a *giant* race and the original inhabitants of Ireland from before the great flood. In one Irish legend the sea rose and drowned most of them after a battle just like Plato's legend of Atlantis. In another Irish legend, Banba, one of the Tuatha Dé Danann arrived in Ireland before the great flood and was said to have been much older then the biblical Noah. There are several other similar pre flood legends in Irish mythology.

United States President Abraham Lincoln made reference to the giants whose '*bones fill the mounds of America*' as did several *New York Times* articles. There are countless legends of a race of red-haired giants from all around the world. Gigantism is caused by the AIP gene and the highest concentration in the world of this 'giant gene' is found in Mid-Ulster where 1 in 150 people carry this DNA.

Gigantism and dwarfism are not genetic mutations - they are genetic memories - expressions from our ancient past

There are numerous records of Irish giants who were over seven-and-a-half-feet tall at a time when the average European was two feet shorter. Many of these giants made their living as show attractions in circuses and carnivals. The bones of Cornelius McGrath, a 7ft 6in man from Country Tipperary who died in 1760 are still held in Trinity College Dublin today.

Patrick Cotter, who adopted the stage name 'O'Brien the Irish Giant', died in 1806. He was one of the few people in history whose height has been verified at over eight feet. In 1972, his remains were excavated and height officially recorded at an incredible 8ft 1in tall.

Charles Byrne was a 7ft 7in giant from County Tyrone in Mid-Ulster. He died in 1783 and his bones are currently displayed in the Hunterian museum in London. DNA extracted from these bones has proven that he carried the AIP 'giant gene'. Height ran in the family. Charles was a relative of the famous Knipe Twins from County Derry, who at 7ft 2in were the tallest identical twins ever recorded.

In 1684, a 7ft-6in-tall Irish giant called Edmund Malone caused a stir in London when he appeared before the court of King Charles II, where the amazed king walked underneath his outstretched arm.

In 1696, James Paris du Plessis recorded meeting a 7ft-tall Irish giantess in London. She was from Portrush in County Antrim, near the world-famous Giants Causeway. In 1701, he spoke to her again in Montpellier, France where the giant lady was a show attraction at a fair. In Irish history, giants go all the way back to the very dawning of time.

The Book of Glendalough (Rawlinson B 502) is stored in the Bodleian Library in Oxford, England. This precious manuscript lists the entire genealogy of the Fomorian giants going right back to before the Biblical Noah, who was said to have been 10 generations removed from Adam and Eve in the *Garden of Eden. Ireland* is known as the *Land of Giants* to this very day and the author is certain there was once a very tall race of people (seven to ten feet tall) in ancient Ireland that became the giants of mythology. The high concentration of the AIP 'giant gene' and the numerous Irish skeletons of people over 7ft-tall support this claim. All around the world we find legends of giants. There is one big difference found in Irish legends - the giants were homegrown, they were *indigenous.*

If I have seen further than others, it is by standing on the shoulders of giants - Issac Newton

The word 'philosophy' literally means the love of wisdom and philosophy is the mother of both science and religion. The Druids were the world's first philosophers and they studied the wisdom of nature, from the smallest creature to the universe itself and everything in-between. Theirs was a scientific religion based on the love of the land that honoured nature in all its glory, its rivers, mountains, oceans, trees, plants, animals, the sun, the moon, the stars and the entire universe in all its splendour. The Druids were skilled in many arts including construction, medicine and astronomy. They considered the sun to be nature's great emblem however they were so much more sophisticated than just sun worshipers or stargazers.

The Druids explored the great laws of nature which they considered to be divine in origin. They taught that the soul was immortal, a spark of the divine fire and that humans were on earth to develop wisdom and virtue in order to evolve and become a star in the heavens. The Greek Pythagoras, who learned from the Abhras the Druid, taught the same philosophy.

The Druids taught people to think for themselves rather than believe dogma. They kept law and order in society and built education systems to teach trades, skills and knowledge. Just like the priests in the Egyptian mystery schools, it took 20 years of dedicated study to become a master Druid.

The Druid mystery schools were the world's first universities and they had both male and female Druids, some of whom were married, others who weren't. The Druids were the 'elders' and had bards and brehons to teach the people, decree laws and settle disputes. For thousands of years a council of chieftains and kings met at the Hill of Tara to decide new laws, making Tara the *real* mother of all parliaments.

The joint highest position in all of Ireland along with the High King was the *Ollamh Érenn.* He or she was the highest Druid in the land and was responsible for the education of the entire Irish people. Each tribe had their own Druid as well as bards (storytellers, poets and historians) and musicians. The harp was considered the most sacred musical instrument - all other instruments were considered inferior. The bards educated and entertained people through songs and stories.

The Druids honoured the T-shaped Tau cross which was a representation of their trinity - the creator, the preserver and the destroyer - three parts of one supreme deity: Mother Nature.

According to *The Celtic Druids* by Godfrey Higgins, the Druids would seek an oak tree with two principal arms and shape them into the form of a T-shaped Tau cross.

On the right hand of this wooden cross the Druids carved the name HESUS.

The T-shaped Tau cross has been associated with many ancient cultures including the Hebrews, Egyptians, Native Americans, Greeks and Romans. T-shaped stones are also found at Gobekli Tepe in Turkey. The early Christian author Tertullian (c 155 - 240 AD) remarked that the T-shaped Tau cross was the shape of cross of Calvary. In Christian circles the Tau cross is known as the Cross of St. Anthony and is also associated with St. Francis of Assisi who adopted it in November 1215 after Pope Innocent III raised the Tau as a symbol of the Christian faith saying: '*The Tau has exactly the same form as the Cross upon which our Lord was crucified on Calvary*'.

This statement by Pope Innocent III has caused no end of trouble for Christian scholars as here we have a Pope, who according to Catholic teachings cannot be wrong in matters of Christian doctrine saying that the Cross of Calvary was really a T-shaped Tau cross, not a Latin † shaped cross. So, either the Pope was wrong, in which case Papal infallibility is not so infallible, or the Pope was right, and Christianity has been worshiping a false idol. Unsurprisingly, the inconvenient issue of the Tau cross has largely been brushed under the carpet.

The Druids also honoured the sun cross ⊕ (also known as the solar cross or sun wheel) which represented the four seasons and the sun's annual progress across the sky. The intersection of the circle and the cross represented the four key times of the year. The top of the sun cross represented the summer solstice, the longest day of the year when the sun reaches its highest point in the sky. The two middle points on either side represent the spring and autumn equinoxes, when there is equal day and night while the lowest point represents the winter solstice: the shortest day of the year when the sun has reached its lowest point in the sky - the *death of the sun* at the winter solstice before it rises again and is reborn on December 25th - the feast of the 'unconquerable sun'.

These ancient Druid teachings were turned into Christian feasts. Christmas is clearly the rebirth of the sun on December 25th as it starts rising again, while Easter is held every year on the first Sunday after the first full moon after March 21st, when the sun has moved into the zodiac sign of *Aries the lamb.* At this time of year (spring or vernal equinox) the days become longer than the nights and new life, such as lambs, are born. Sun worship and Astrology, also known as astro-theology, are at the very root of most major religions who usually still worship on the day of the sun - Sunday.

At one time the Druids were highly organised teachers who travelled all over the world sowing the seeds of civilisation. Their involvement in the development of civilisation has been largely airbrushed out of history by the Romans, among others, who did whatever they could to destroy all memory of the Druids. The ignorant have always attacked the wise and for centuries the Romans attacked learning with a vengeance.

It is no great secret that the Romans undertook to destroy all records of the old world in order to promote their new 'holy empire' which they believed gave them the divine right to conquer (slaughter) the entire world. There were no limits to Christian fury directed against places of learning and anyone who didn't submit entirely to Christian dogma was labelled a pagan.

The most famous seat of learning in the ancient world was the Great Library of Alexandria in Egypt and its destruction was one of the greatest crimes ever committed against humanity. Close to one million precious scrolls from the ancient world were destroyed setting humanity back thousands of years. Many scholars view this atrocity as the birth of a dark age of ignorance where people were not allowed to think for themselves. In reality however, the destruction of the great library was only the tip of the iceberg.

Arles in the south of France contained an ancient seat of learning that was founded by the Druids around 2,000 BC. This site, which was around 1,700 years older than the Great Library of Alexandria, contained many precious records and priceless artefacts from the ancient world. This Druid college was completely destroyed by a Christian mob who attacked it in 270 AD.

In 389 AD, another Druid college in Bibrate, France was also destroyed by a Christian mob. This college had an astonishing 40,000 students and offered courses in philosophy, literature, grammar, law, medicine, astronomy, architecture and religion.

All around the world we find the same pattern of destruction which gives us just a glimpse of the overwhelming hatred of learning held by the ignorant masses as the world sunk into a dark age of ignorance. Fear, guilt, shame and hatred were the weapons of mass destruction as numerous pagan sites and buildings were Christianised. Ireland's Druid monasteries were converted into Christian monasteries while her pagan deities such as Brigit were declared saints by the new world religion. This same pattern was repeated all over the globe.

The cleaner something is, the easier to dirty it and the Romans undertook a campaign to destroy the reputation of the Irish Druids, even claiming they practiced human sacrifice. There is very little evidence for human sacrifice in Ireland however there is any amount of evidence for human sacrifice in the Vatican. Since its very foundation, thousands of scholars and alternative thinkers were boiled alive in animal fat, torn limb from limb or burnt at the stake for daring to question church dogma. The last human sacrifice officially performed on behalf of the Vatican was in 1826 with the execution of schoolteacher Cayetano Ripoll as part of the Inquisition, for apparently teaching Deism (that God is Nature) in his school. Actions speak louder than words.

Women were about the only thing the Christians hated more than knowledge, which was yet another reason to destroy the Druids, many of whom were female. The Romans sought to destroy all record of the Druids to hide the great skeleton in their closet:

That all the world's religions and civilisation had their roots in one fertile mother soil - Irish Druidism.

The author J.R.R. Tolkien was heavily influenced by Irish mythology when writing his *Lord of the Rings* epic. His wizards were based on the Irish Druids, while the elves were based on the Tuatha Dé Dannan.

The Tuatha Dé Dannan were a highly advanced people who according to one legend arrived in Ireland in *ships from the sky*. They are considered in Irish mythology as a divine but mortal race who bought advanced knowledge, skills, music and poetry to the people. Most of Ireland's great cultural heroes were DéDananns and they were also described as being 'the men of science who were gods'. An old Irish poem says of the magical DéDananns:

The truth was not known beneath the sky of stars, whether they were of heaven or of earth.

The wandering DéDananns are described as being tall and beautiful with pale skin, red or blonde hair and blue or green eyes. This description matches the numerous red or fair-haired mummies found all around the world and also matches the description of Cro-Magnon man who had giant brains 20% bigger than modern day humans.

They were known as the wandering DéDananns because they travelled the world.

There is no mistaking the monuments of the ancient Irish that are found all around the planet. Mounds, cairns, dolmens and stone circles have been found in virtually every country on earth and were built by the same people who bought the gifts of civilisation to early man - the *megalithic mother culture*. These sowers of civilisation travelled the entire world not to build an empire, but to push the human race forward. Ireland was the first mistress of the sea who bought light and learning to a dark barbaric world. Hers was a mission of mercy.

Ireland's mysterious round towers have been the cause of much debate and disagreement for centuries. No historian really knows when they were built, who built them or why. In the 19th century they were considered pagan Druid towers. In the 20th century they were considered Christian. In all of Ireland's historical records there is not a single account of a round tower having ever being built. Thankfully, the author can put an end to this debate once and for all.

Ireland's round towers were built with a form of mortar which contains horsehair which was added to mortar to bind it together and to prevent cracking. *This horsehair can be carbon-dated* to provide an accurate age for the mysterious round towers once and for all and this knowledge has already been passed on to the Irish monuments service who have confirmed that they intend carbon-dating some of Ireland's round towers.

Time will tell how old the towers really are and when their true age is established it will send a shockwave around the entire world. The author suspects they will become known internationally as the round towers of Atlantis.

The one duty we owe to history is to rewrite it

- Oscar Wilde

The huge entrance stone at Newgrange which weighs 5 tons was transported 30km to the site by boat

An Irish round tower at Clondalkin, Dublin. Carbon-dating the horsehair used in its mortar can prove it true age

CONCLUSION

Most people would rather die than think
- Bertrand Russell

The author is satisfied that this book proves beyond all reasonable doubt that the ancient Irish were an Atlantic mother culture that sowed the seeds of civilisation around the world and that every country on earth, not just Ireland, has a spectacular ancient history that has been all but forgotten.

The contents of this book are groundbreaking and its implications are enormous. This writing could be the ravings of a madman, the work of a genius, or anything in-between so do not believe a word you read, just do your own research and most importantly do your thinking. The truth does not need a salesman and it's very easy to spot a false prophet, they ask you to believe them.

All great ideas are first ridiculed, then attacked, then accepted and the author does not expect the ideas in this book to be accepted in his lifetime, nor does he expect a rational debate on the points raised. Too many reputations are at stake and this work goes completely against mainstream opinion, yet a scholar has to do what a scholar has to do. The current version of history is a house of cards that's about to come crumbling down and the trickle of evidence for an Atlantic mother culture has become a river that the mainstream has yet to join.

This book has been written for the freethinkers of today, the scholars of tomorrow and generations not yet born. It's dedicated to the memory of true scholars like Hypatia, Bruno, Galileo and thousands of others who were persecuted by ignorant men with a thirst for blood, a hatred of learning and a love of power.

The author has often wondered what our ancient ancestors would think of our modern world. He suspects they would be amazed by our technology, impressed by our progress and horrified by our lack of humanity. It's time to face the truth. Everything is backwards. Everything is upside down. Doctors destroy health, lawyers destroy justice, universities destroy knowledge, governments destroy freedom, media destroys truth, religions destroy spirituality, empires destroy civilisation and humans destroy earth.

Humanity has clearly reached a crossroads. One road leads to extinction, the other to evolution and there is no turning back. We must all learn the lessons of history or we are doomed to repeat them, and Mother Earth has shaken many species off her back. As a species, we are drowning in information and starving for wisdom.

As we slowly climb out of the slime of ignorance, we quickly develop new technology with the potential to either build a better world or destroy it. Yet there is hope in all this chaos and hope springs eternal.

A golden age of light follows every age of darkness and the next age will be a golden age - *an age of wisdom.*

The birth of a new age marks the death of an old one and the empires built during the Dark Ages are dying.

It's time to reclaim the lost light.

During the Dark Ages a great mirror of truth was smashed into a thousand pieces and many things that were lost have yet to be found. Slowly but surely the pieces are being put back together. Nature works in mysterious ways. Sometimes when things seem to be falling apart, they are really falling into place.

Éirinn go Brách
(For the Honour of Ireland)

REFERENCES

The supreme purpose of history is a better world
- Herbert Hoover

For your convenience all online references have been reduced to a shortened weblink.

INTRODUCTION

Plato's Timaeus *shorturl.at/vMNZ8*

Plato's Critias *shorturl.at/cdiRS*

Younger Dryas: *shorturl.at/cA469*

Ancestors of Egypt: L. A. Waddell, *Makers of Civilization in Race and History*, (1929) and L. A. Waddell, *Egyptian Origins.*

Atlantis from a Geographer's Perspective: Ulf Erlingsson, *Atlantis from a Geographer's Perspective* (Lindorm Publishing, 2004).

Newgrange: Geraldine Stout, *Newgrange and the Bend of the Boyne* (Cork University Press, 2004).

Man sailed to Australia 65,000 years ago: *New York Times,* shorturl.at/dnwAX

Rarest genetic combination on earth: *Medical Xpress,* shorturl.at/jFSX2

Red-haired Ramesses II mummy: *Madain Project,* shorturl.at/fCGK9

Precession of the Equinox: shorturl.at/hknS9

Druid stone circles: Joseph Gwilt, *An Encyclopaedia of Architecture* (Cambridge University Press, 2014)

Hyperborea: shorturl.at/wABMO

Druid college destruction: Tom Harpur, *The Pagan Christ: Recovering the Lost Light* P61 (Thomas Allen Publishers, 2004).

Irish Tailtean Games: T.H.Nalley, *The Aeonac Tailteann and The Tailteann Games* (The Talbot Press Ltd. Dublin,1922)

EGYPT

Sunset Land, Urani, Menes' empty Egyptian tomb, Menes buried in Ireland: All references to these are found in: L. A. Waddell, *Makers of Civilization in Race and History*, (1929) and L. A. Waddell, *Egyptian Origins.*

Arrived from the Atlantic around 12,000 years ago: This is 9850 BC on the Turin Papyrus. N.Zhirov, *Atlantis: Atlantology Basic Problems*, (The Minerva Group, 2001).

Scotia's grave in County Kerry: Geoffrey Keating, *The History of Ireland, From the Earliest Period to the English Invasion.* p.202 (Making of America Books, 1866, translated by John O'Mahony). Maeve Friel, *Here Lies: A Guide to Irish Graves* (Poolbeg, 1997)

Egyptian faience beads: *shorturl.at/orst0*

Skull of a Barbary ape: *shorturl.at/coACD*

The Nabta Playa: *shorturl.at/JSTV2*

Mounds in Egyptian writings: *shorturl.at/kzMNZ*

Benben mound: *shorturl.at/ehCK4*

Atum Mound: Pyramid Texts, Utterances 587 and 600, Atum himself is at times referred to as 'mound'

The Second Sphinx: *shorturl.at/hmpwY*

Lost Labyrinth of Egypt: *shorturl.at/gkmwX*

Red-haired genetics: *shorturl.at/kpx34*

Ginger the mummy: *shorturl.at/fY346*

Ramesses II has red hair: *shorturl.at/cjkFL*

The Egyptian Book of the Dead: The twentieth prayer of the 141st chapter of the ancient *Egyptian Book of the Dead*, is dedicated 'to the Goddess greatly beloved, with red hair' - E. A. W. Budge, *The Book of the Dead.*

Pharaoh Tutankhamun's haplogroup: Tutankhamun's DNA - RM269. *shorturl.at/ghADM*

GREECE

Hyperborea: Diodorus Siculus, Library of History (Loeb Classical Library,1935) *shorturl.at/klrCZ*

Hyperborea mythology: *shorturl.at/asDK0*

Irish Boreadach: *shorturl.at/klGR5*

Tuatha DéDanann: *shorturl.at/gNO34 shorturl.at/nostU*

Abaris the Hyperborean: *The Round Towers of Ireland* by Henry O'Brien. *shorturl.at/jkAJ9*

Irish Tailtean Games: *The Aeonac Tailteann and The Tailteann Games* (The Talbot Press Ltd. Dublin,1922) *shorturl.at/dqvGX*

Hercules Golden Apples: *shorturl.at/hEXY7*

Atlas in Hyperborea: *shorturl.at/dAQUY*

Hyperboreans: *shorturl.at/dBFR1*

Wolves and Swans of Hyperborea: *shorturl.at/fIV19*

Achilles funeral mound: *shorturl.at/rsKX0*

Irish Wolfhound: *shorturl.at/gkGM0*

Garden of Hesperides in Hyperborea: *shorturl.at/lIV06*

Golden apples of the Hesperides in Irish annals: *shorturl.at/ijEIV*

Hercules visited Hyperborea: *shorturl.at/suB17*

The Druids: Godfrey Higgins, *The Celtic Druids* (Cosimo Classics, 2007) p. 121 *shorturl.at/almBW*

Destruction of Arles: Tom Harpur, *The Pagan Christ: Recovering the Lost Light* P61 (Thomas Allen Publishers, 2004).

Orpheus*: shorturl.at/jvzA7*

Atlas: shorturl.at/cvC46

Atalanta Golden Apples: *shorturl.at/cmrB7*

Hermes: *shorturl.at/osT36*

Hermes cairns: *shorturl.at/MST01*

Emerald tablets: *shorturl.at/atEFM*

Ireland and Mauritania: Edward Lipinski, *Orientalia Lovaniensia Analecta: Itineraria Phoenicia* p 462, (Peeters Publishers, 2004).

Atlas, king of two separate places: *shorturl.at/tFGO1*

The Eye of the Sahara: *shorturl.at/bimyA*

Cerne: Hanno, Thomas Falconer, *The Voyage of Hanno: Translated, and Accompanied with the Greek Text* (T. Cadell, jun. and Davies, 1797.)

The Amazons: *shorturl.at/prFM1*

Phaethon: *shorturl.at/MRSW0*

Missing fifth planet: *shorturl.at/enrB9*

The sea rose drowning most: *shorturl.at/dOY69*

Ireland tsunamis: *shorturl.at/psBSW shorturl.at/suQS9*

Comet impact in the Atlantic Ocean: Otto Muck, *The Secret of Atlantis* (Collins, 1978). *shorturl.at/vCORW*

Nasa comment: *shorturl.at/puxE7*

The Storegga Slides: *shorturl.at/bvU15*

Doggerland: *shorturl.at/gDILN*

14,000 year old antler: *shorturl.at/dsBEZ*

Gulf Stream didn't stop during the Ice Age: *shorturl.at/jxIOZ*

Giants of Hyperborea: *shorturl.at/knuyY*

Fir Bolg enslavement: *shorturl.at/ksyFT*

Battle of Ventry: *Battle of Ventry P238 , 257, specific reference to Greece, shorturl.at/JKPX7*

AFRICA

Brú na Bóinne: Geraldine Stout, *Newgrange and the Bend of the Boyne* (Cork University Press, 2004).

The Eye of the Sahara: *shorturl.at/svCMT*

African Humid period: *shorturl.at/jt049*

The Amazons: *shorturl.at/prFM1*

Fénius Farsaid: *shorturl.at/bsBDT*

Radar images of the Mauritanian desert: *shorturl.at/mnwY1 shorturl.at/wARV6*

Berbers are of Irish descent: *The Tribes of Northern and Central Kordofan* (C.U.P. Archive, 1967) p. 90.

Ancient Irish and Berber language: Markku Filppula, Juhani Klemola, Heli Paulasto, *English and Celtic in Contact* (Routledge, 2008) p 80.

King Solomon's goldmines: *shorturl.at/mxDSZ*

Sand and gravel deposits: *shorturl.at/houvL*

Ancient irrigation systems: *shorturl.at/lpBC8*

Early large-scaled human conflict: *shorturl.at/ptyJP*

Remains of the giant Antaeus: Plutarch, *Delphi Complete Works of Plutarch,* (Delphi Classics, 2013)

The city of Formia in Italy: *shorturl.at/ertNU*

Geoffrey of Monmouth: Geoffrey of Monmouth, *The History of the Kings of Britain.* (Lewis Thorpe, trans. London: Peguin Books, 1966.) p 172-75.

The world's oldest stone tools: *shorturl.at/fluz2*

ASIA

Man sailed to Australia 65,000 years ago: *shorturl.at/auX06*

NZ Maori encountered first inhabitants: *shorturl.at/cgiFJ*

Uru-Kehu: Gayle Redfern, *Ancient Wisdoms, Exploring the Mysteries and Connections* (AuthorHouse, 2009)

Cherchen Man: *shorturl.at/dfsAO*

Red-haired Chinese mummies: *Mair, Victor H. Mummies of the Tarim Basin (1995Archaeology) 48 (2): 28–35;*

Standing stones giants: *shorturl.at/yCER8*

Dolmens giants: *shorturl.at/fmEY5*

50,000 megaliths were destroyed: Brad Olsen, *Sacred Places Around the World* (CCC Publishing, 2004), p 232.

The Irish language is remarkably similar to ancient Hebrew, Chaldean, Arabic and Sanskrit: Lt. General Charles Vallancey, *Dictionary of the Language of the Aire Coti* (Graisbury and Campbell, 1802). *shorturl.at/arwPS*

Ogham writing on the Shigar Idol: *shorturl.at/fsNST*

Edmund Spencer: Edmund Spencer, *The Works of Edmund Spencer* (Washbourne, 1845) p. 491.

The 'Golden Island' of the Sanskrit texts: Lt. General Charles Vallancey, *Dictionary of the Language of the Aire Coti* (Graisbury and Campbell, 1802). *shorturl.at/arwPS*

Three Hindu deities travelled to Svetadvipa on a chariot of swans: Walter Eugene Clark, *Śākadvīpa and Śvetadvīpa*, Journal of the American Oriental Society, Vol. 39 (1919), pp. 209-242 (American Oriental Society)

Indian musical instruments have Irish roots: *shorturl.at/glRWX*

Hanging Gardens of Babylon: *shorturl.at/tABIV*

Hanging Gardens are located in Mosul: *shorturl.at/wHKN5 shorturl.at/fnqtT shorturl.at/eyFO9*

Magh an alternative to the word draoi : Henry O'Brien, *Phoenecian Ireland* (Longman, 1833) p 253.

Meltwater Pulse 1B: *shorturl.at/jGQZ7*

AMERICA

Bluefish Caves: *shorturl.at/alCM0*

Pre-Clovis culture: *shorturl.at/djkAR*

A giant dolmen: Barry Fell, *America B.C.* (Artisan Publishers, 2008).

The Duhare Tribe: *shorturl.at/mD026*

Rock carvings similar to those found in Ireland: *shorturl.at/mpFQY*

Chinchorro mummies: *shorturl.at/kyIMP*

Spanish records of red-haired tribes: Xaviant Haze, *Ancient Giants of the Americas* (Red Wheel/Weiser, 2016)

Names written on Irish ogham stones: *shorturl.at/bfinY*

Dr Barry Fell, Harvard: *shorturl.at/bchEY*

Rock dust… from 1000 BC: Carl Lehrburger: *Secrets of Ancient America* (Bear and Co. 2015).

Abraham Lincoln giants: *shorturl.at/dghCH*

New York Times giant article from 1897: *shorturl.at/bdFI5*

New York Times giant article from 1886: *shorturl.at/lsJ12*

Giant gene is found in Mid-Ulster: *shorturl.at/lDHNQ*

EUROPE

Greywacke stone: *shorturl.at/bkvLN*

Brú na Bóinne: Geraldine Stout, *Newgrange and the Bend of the Boyne* (Cork University Press, 2004).

Faroe Islands: *shorturl.at/ouFLX*

A primitive musical whistle: *shorturl.at/bdehN*

Big brained Cro-Magnons: *shorturl.at/intwZ*

The Guanches: *shorturl.at/iEJZ2*

Atlantic Europeans: *shorturl.at/lEFKR*

Genetic Haplogroup R1b: Anatole A. Klyosov, *DNA Genealogy*, (Scientific Research Publishing, 2018).

Ireland has the highest concentration of R1b on earth: *shorturl.at/crwU1*

Hypatia of Alexandria: *shorturl.at/imxF8*

Laudibilter: *shorturl.at/gpVY9 shorturl.at/BCQ47*

BRITAIN

Britain's slave trade: *shorturl.at/kCSU0*

The Penal Laws: *shorturl.at/glEPW*

Food Removal: Chris Fogarty, *Ireland 1845 – 1850: The Perfect Holocaust and Who Kept it "Perfect"* (Fogarty Publishing, 2018).

Edmund Spencer: *shorturl.at/xCV14 shorturl.at/nBJ17*

Stonehenge legends: Patricia Monaghan, *The Encyclopedia of Celtic Mythology and Folklore* (Facts on File, 2008)

Credible British Source: Geoffrey of Monmouth, *The History of the Kings of Britain*, c. 1136

Dronehenge: shorturl.at/pxFZ6

IRELAND

Stone Age quay: shorturl.at/orstF

Stone tools in Mell in Drogheda: shorturl.at/bkBYZ

The Shining Face of Lugh - the Sun God: T.W.Rolleston, *Myths & Legends of the Celtic Race* (George G. Harrap & Company 1911)

Oldest solar eclipse ever recorded: shorturl.at/emoyS

Precession of the Equinox: shorturl.at/gjCKO

Ireland was never completely frozen over: shorturl.at/vxyNV shorturl.at/fFKOX

Puerto Rico Trench: shorturl.at/bHKNS

Otto Muck: Otto Muck, *The Secret of Atlantis* (Collins, 1978), p 151. shorturl.at/ioEM5

Old Stone Age finds - Mell Drogheda: *shorturl.at/jsCNU* **County Down:** *shorturl.at/hNOS4* **Inishmore:** *shorturl.at/pqryO*

12,500 year old bear bone: *shorturl.at/lpMST*

4,000 year old bog butter: *shorturl.at/cZ469*

Lactose Tolerance: *shorturl.at/fnrE4*

Irish Hobby horse: *shorturl.at/pv569 shorturl.at/vxJO7*

In one Irish legend the sea rose: *shorturl.at/myJUW shorturl.at/hyLU5*

Before and after the Great Flood: James McKillop, *A Dictionary of Celtic Mythology* (Oxford University Press, 1998)

Banba - before the flood: *shorturl.at/rJS17 shorturl.at/fHVZ2 shorturl.at/fgiR2*

Fintan - before the flood: *shorturl.at/cnW09*

Irish Giant gene: *shorturl.at/ltJTY*

The immortal soul: *The Religion of the Ancient Celts* (Library of Alexandria, 2010).

20 years to become a master druid: *shorturl.at/afzL9*

Druids on the hill Of Tara: *shorturl.at/LNSX5*

Ollamh Érenn: *shorturl.at/apLR6*

Cayetano Ripoll: *shorturl.at/BCOS3*

Tolkien Lord of the Rings: *shorturl.at/syHK7*

Tuatha DéDanann: *shorturl.at/gNO34 shorturl.at/nostU*

History is written by the winners

- Napoleon

INDEX

A

B

G

H

I

J

K

L

M

N

O

P

R

S

T

U

V

W

Y

KEYSTONE
UNIVERSITY

MISSION

THE WORLD'S BEST UNIVERSITY

Our mission is to build the world's best university - a centre of excellence that pushes the human race forward

This is Keystone

www.keystone.ie

Printed in Great Britain
by Amazon

50779489R00096